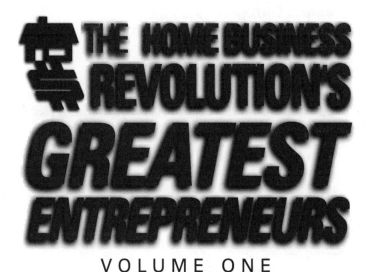

VOLUME ONE

The exclusive interviews from
Six-Figure Income Magazine

by **GERY CARSON**
with **Jan Wallen**

The Home Business Revolution's Greatest Entrepreneurs
By Gery Carson

Printed in the United States of America

ISBN 0-9669615-0-1

Published by
Carson Services, Inc.
P.O. Box 4785, Lincoln, NE 68504
(402) 434-8480

DEDICATION

To my father, Kenley. *Kind, gentle, humble, and always a friendly smile, you brightened the world. And though you may have thought I wasn't paying attention to the values you taught by example throughout your life: service to God, service to country, grace, commitment, honesty, hard work, respect...I was. Today they are my values, Dad. Tomorrow, I will pass them on to my children. Thank you, Dad. I love you.*

CONTENTS

INTRODUCTION

I still remember it clearly. It was 1985, I was 23, and I had just discovered two books that would go on to have a huge impact on my life and the business I was about to start.

The first book was *The Magic of Thinking Big* by David J. Schwartz. That book opened my eyes, and the other, the all-time success classic, *Think and Grow Rich* by Napoleon Hill, sent me *soaring* with the knowledge that I had within me spectacular, untapped talents and unlimited potential.

I was also very inspired by Mr. Hill's mission – to interview the richest, most successful people in the world, and to document what it was they had in common, so that this knowledge could be shared with anyone who had the drive and desire to achieve greatness.

In 1998, when I began formulating ideas for a new magazine that I wanted to publish, my "old friend" *Think and Grow Rich* emerged in my thinking. I knew instantly what I wanted to do. Like Napoleon Hill, I would shine a light on ultra-successful entrepreneurs, so that others could learn from them and apply that knowledge to their lives and businesses.

In your hands you hold detailed profiles of 17 incredible and very successful individuals. Indeed! Laid out for you to emulate are the very strategies, philosophies, and actual techniques they used to achieve their mammoth success – a literal wealth of ideas, insights, and guidance by the best of the best. *Enjoy!*

Gery Carson

Robert Blackman

Age: 36

Family: Wife, Karyn (married in 1984), and Daughter, Kelley Ann, age 2

Education: Bachelors in Business Administration 1984 Oklahoma State University

Employees: 4

Type of Business: Network marketing author and distributor. Also does consulting, copywriting, design, and printing.

Year Started in Business: 1987

Best month (gross revenue): $85,000

Hours worked per week during start-up: 60-80

Hours worked per week now: 10-20

Heros: Father (he served in Germany during WWII), Rich DeVos & Jay Van Andel (for cutting the path in the Network Marketing forest)

Favorite Business Periodicals: *Robb Report, Upline Magazine, Jay Abraham's Newsletter*

Favorite Business Books/Authors: *Dig Your Well Before You're Thirsty* by Harvey McKay, *Advertising Magic* by Brian Keith Voiles, *Personal Power* by Tony Robbins

Relaxes by: Playing Golf

Favorite part of his business: Helping his downline make money!

Least favorite part of his business: The frustration of seeing people so close to success but who won't do the necessary things it takes to get there –when it becomes apparent that you can't help someone because of his or her negative mindset.

Stays in shape by: lifting weights in his own office gym. Golfs at least twice weekly and uses a treadmill daily.

Admired Companies: Microsoft, Amway, Longevity Network

Favorite Quotes:

"You Make The Rules" (Jay Abraham)

"What If Everybody In Your Downline Duplicated EXACTLY What You Did Every Single Day Of The Week, Would You Be Excited Or Would You Be Depressed?" (Robert Blackman)

"The Big Shots Are Only The Little Shots Who Keep On Shooting" (Christopher Morley)

Books, Tapes & Reports By Robert Blackman

BOOKS:
- How To Sit Back & Get Rich In MLM
- How To 100% Absolutely Guarantee That You Make Money In Network Marketing

AUDIOS:
- How I Went From Bankruptcy In 1990 To $100,000 In 1995 Through Network Marketing
- How To Select The Right MLM Company, Product, Service & Sponsor
- How To Find Eager Prospects For Your Business
- Using Direct Mail To Promote Your MLM
- The 10 Most Common Network Marketing Mistakes & How You Can Avoid Them
- How One Full Page Ad Changed My Life Forever
- How I Built A Downline Of 2,000 People In Only 9 Months

- How To Use The Telephone To Build Your MLM
- Managing Multiple Income Streams
- Protege Bootcamp
- Guaranteed Check Program
- Are You Fishing For Whales, Or Are You Fishing For Minnows?
- Putting It All Together & Staying Motivated

VIDEOS:
- Why Retailing & Warm Marketing Are Making A Comeback
- Never Quit - How I Stayed Motivated When Things Weren't Working
- MLM Mastery Course

Call (405) 360-6300 Ext. 806 from your fax-on-demand for a complete price list. Or, call or fax my office for a free catalog.

Robert Blackman's books and tapes can also be purchased on the internet at:www.networkmarketing.com/bookstore/

Father Was Inspiration

For **Robert Blackman**, it was dad who served as the inspiration for entering business. "My Father was the president of a continuous forms business in Bartlesville, Oklahoma called Central States Business Forms. At age 58 he took early retirement and started a quick-print franchise. At the time I was 18. It really impressed me that dad was willing to "start over" at age 58 because he was tired of all the corporate politics. He left a $75,000 a year job in 1980 (which was big back then) and started over."

Robert had grown up in his dad's manufacturing plan. At age 25, it was time to follow his lead and start his own business. And as if to prove the value of his upbringing, Robert turned a profit in his very first month and has never looked back.

Like most entrepreneurs, the reward is freedom. "Some days I don't work at all. Other days I work 18 hours straight. It just depends on how I feel," says Robert. Being able to write his own paycheck ranks high, too. "The only limit to the amount of money I make is up to me! I love getting up in the morning and being in complete control of my financial destiny." ■

*Robert Blackman gets his message
across during one of his seminars*

Thomas DeRosa

Age: 23

Family: Wife, Suzanne, and daughter, Hailey, 3

Employees: 0

Type of Business: Network Marketing

Year Started in Business: 1995

Best month (gross revenue): $15,000

Hours worked per week during start-up: 15 (while still a full-time college student)

Hours worked per week now: 15-50

Favorite Business Periodicals: *Barron's, Business Week, Fortune*

Favorite Business Books/Authors: *The Road Ahead* by Bill Gates, Brian Tracy

Relaxes by: Reading, traveling or watching movies (a favorite being *Braveheart*)

Favorite part of his business: Working at home

Least favorite part of his business: Bookkeeping

Stays in shape by: Daily push-ups and sit-ups, snowboarding in the winter and playing tennis in the summer.

Admired Companies: Oracle, Microsoft, Alpine Industries

Favorite Quotes:

"There's no point in carrying the ball if you don't know where the goal is." (Mitchell Tolle)

"I will...until." (Brian Tracy)

He Gave Up His Degree To Pursue Independence

Thomas DeRosa boldly demonstrated his commitment to succeeding in his own business while still in college at the University of Connecticut. In his final semester of a four-year pursuit of a degree in Industrial Psychology/Business, while carrying honor status no less, Thomas dropped out to pursue his network marketing career with Alpine Industries.

Income, or in Thomas' case, a lack of income, played a major role in his decision. "I was completely broke, and I needed some immediate income. But the truth is, I never wanted to rely on my degree for a job, and I was looking to start my own business."

Most parents would have fought such a decision by a child; Thomas' mother did not. Because of that support, "for believing in me even when I dropped out of college," Thomas today considers his mother the person who has most influenced his life.

Other influences that helped Thomas achieve success in network marketing include his daughter, Hailey. "Her early addition into my life forced me to push harder." Thomas also credits Bob Giddens, his upline in Alpine, for teaching him about goalsetting and how network marketing works.

If you ask Thomas about his motivation, he'll tell you it's being in complete control of his own success. "Doing what I want, when I want, especially in terms of spending time with my family."

Heros include Larry Ellison, CEO of Oracle. "He started out in life as a poor city boy, and through hard work, built the second largest software company in the world. I admire the ways he runs his company, forges alliances, and how one of his goals is to beat my second hero, Bill Gates!" Another hero is Mitchell Tolle, "for following and achieving his dream of becoming a world-renowned artist in his own time, in an industry where so few ever accomplish such a task. He epitomizes persistence."

At the age of just 23, Thomas' own successes have been remarkable. He turned his first profit in just his second month. His own network of Alpine distributors now numbers over 1200. And he was recently selected by Mike Jackson, the co-owner of Alpine to become one of the first 50 people to reach Alpine's top rank, Master Manager. Not bad for a college drop-out. ■

Rick Eriksen

Age: 40

Family: Single

Education: 2 years college

Employees: 0

Type of Business: Network Marketing

Market: People who seek financial independence

Year Started in Business: 1982

Best month (gross revenue): $36,000

Hours worked per week during start-up: 30

Hours worked per week now: 30

Favorite Business Periodicals: *ENTREPRENEUR Magazine, SUCCESS Magazine, SIX-FIGURE INCOME Magazine*

Favorite Business Authors: Anthony Robbins, Brian Tracy, Dr. John Gray

Relaxes by: Playing golf, snow-skiing, sailing, watching movies and college football

Favorite part of his business: Talking to new people interested in what he markets.

Least favorite part of his business: Cold callers pitching him on their programs.

Stays in shape by: Walking 6 miles per day, four days a week, also lifting weights for an hour after each walk.

Admired Companies: The Peoples Network, Carson Services, Inc., and Cutting Edge Media Group.

Favorite Quotes:

"If it's going to be, it's up to me."

"Whatever it takes!"

"Never, ever, never, ever give up!"

Eriksen Models Success After His Heroes

Rick Eriksen has been entrepreneurial for most of his life, starting his first business at just 17 years of age. His current company, DYNA*STAR MARKETING, was launched in 1982 and took just six months to turn its first profit.

He models his success after his dad. "He came to the USA in 1950 as an immigrant from Lithuania with no formal education and raised 5 children and became a millionnaire. Everything he did, he did for his family. I aspire to one day be as good a man as my father. My dad is the best man I have ever known."

Troy Aikman, former UCLA quarterback and now Dallas Cowboy, is another one of Rick's heros. "Troy is a hero to me because he is one of the best there is in football but also because of his willingness to give back to the community. His charitable work is renowned and his successful track record is well documented."

Besides large-scale success as a network marketer, Rick has also notched over $100,000 in Commercial Investment Real Estate. And on a personal note, Rick recently lost 110 pounds in seven months and has successfully kept that weight off for the past year.

Rick's story would not be complete without mentioning Tony Robbins, the renowned personal development coach and the man Rick says most influenced his life. "I used to work for Tony and he always said, *find people who are successful in what you want to do, and then do what they do. Model them.*" ∎

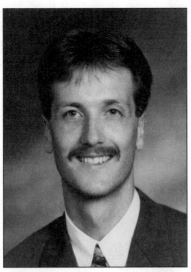

Charles Leslie

Age: 30

Family: Wife, Deanna

Education: 4-yr. College Graduate, B.A. Business

Employees: 0

Type of Business: Network Marketing

Year Started in Business: 1991

Best month (gross revenue): $12,200

Hours worked per week during start-up: 50

Hours worked per week now: 45-50

Heros: Bill McCarthey of Promise Keepers, Billy Graham, Dr. James Dobson and Gary Bauer

Favorite Business Periodicals: *Working at Home, MLM Insider, Money Maker's Monthly*

Favorite Business Books/ Authors: Anthony Robbins

Relaxes by: Taking walks in the beautiful Pacific Northwest. Also, trips to the ocean and the San Juan Islands.

Favorite part of his business: The challenge of taking himself to the highest limits of his potential, being creative and seeing people's lives change in a positive way as they break out of their comfort zones, work hard and reach their dreams.

Least favorite part of his business: Working with people who treat their business like a hobby and at the same time expect success without time and effort.

Stays in shape by: Working out at a local athletic club five days a week, utilizing primarily the stationary bike, stair climber, and treadmill.

Admired Companies: The Peoples Network, a company whose mission is to bring positive TV programming and personal growth into one million homes by the year 2000.

Passion, Purpose & Integrity Drive Charles Leslie

Unlike most Business Majors he knew, **Charles Leslie** was not interested in getting a job working for a corporation and being limited to a 9-5 schedule. "I was fascinated and intrigued by the possiblities of living the American Dream - the dream of being my own boss and being financially free," Charles explains. But where to start? Initially, Charles looked into real estate. Entrepreneurial magazines picked up at the newstand further fueled his search for a business of his own. Eventually, Charles would discover network marketing. "When I was introduced to network marketing I knew that this would be my vehicle to reaching my dreams of being my own boss and having financial and time freedom."

He was right. Today, that network marketing business not only employs Charles but also his wife, Deanna. Working side by side, their income now easily tops $100,000 a year. So that others could learn from his success, Charles also now teaches network marketing at colleges in the Pacific Northwest.

What drives Charles Leslie? The opportunity to create a life instead of making a living tops the benefits list for Charles. "Building a walk-a-way residual income business is very rewarding and gives me the time and money to pursue my passions which include starting a ministry dedicated to inspiring, equiping, and educating individuals to rise up, take action, and utilize their God-given potential to live lives full of passion, purpose, and integrity."

Charles points out, however, that it wasn't quite an overnight success. "I started in December of 1992 with a $32 check." But within six months, that $32 check had climbed to $1000 and the Leslie's were looking at their first real profit.

Charles credits his parents with instilling in him the attitude to succeed in business. "My parents have been so influential, they have loved me unconditionally and encouraged me to be my best. They were so dedicated to my success that when I decided to play on a hockey team in Seattle (1 1/2 hours away) that they drove me to all of the games and practices (five days a week, 8 months out of the year for three years). Specifically, my mother and father taught me about how to present myself. My mom, being from England, always reminded me to speak well and my dad always kept sure that I was presenting myself as someone with purpose and direction."

Those influences were invaluable when a health crisis developed. "There were days when the prognosis for my improved health were dim," remembers Charles. Scripture further strengthened his hope, especially a verse from Isaiah 40:31, "but those who hope in the Lord will renew their strength. They will soar on wings like eagles; they will run and not grow weary, they will walk and not be faint." So moved by these words was Charles, he later rechristened his company, "Eagle Flight Enterprises." ∎

Joe Rubino

Age: 41

Family: Wife Janice

Education: Doctorate, DMD degree

Employees: Zero, one business partner, Dr. Tom Ventullo

Type of Business: Network Marketing

Best month (gross revenue): $62,000

Hours worked per week during start-up: 10-15 while still maintaining his dental practice for 3 years.

Hours worked per week now: About 30

Favorite Business Magazines: *Success, Upline Magazine, Working at Home*

Favorite Business Books/Authors:
• *The Greatest Networker in the World* by John Fogg
• *Seven Habits of Highly Effective People* by Stephen Covey

• *Awaken The Giant Within* by Tony Robbins

Relaxes by: Playing golf, listening to music, driving his Triumph TR6, reading

Favorite part of his business: Impacting the lives of others. Helping people see that they can do anything they desire as long as they believe in themselves.

Least favorite part of his business: Not being able to always help those with negative attitudes and those who don't expect success.

Stays in shape by: Playing golf, roller blading, ice skating, skiing.

Admired Companies: Oxyfresh Worldwide, Microsoft, Disney

Favorite Quotes:

"Security is mostly a superstition. It does not exist in nature nor do the children of men as a whole experience it. Avoiding danger is no safer in the long run than outright exposure. Life is either a daring adventure or nothing." (Helen Keller)

"This is the true joy in life, being used for a purpose recognized by yourself as a mighty one; being a force of nature instead of a feverish, selfish little clod of ailments and grievances complaining that the world will not devote itself to making you happy. I am of the opinion that my life belongs to the whole community and as long as I live, it is my privilege to do for it whatever I can. I want to be thoroughly used up when I die, for the harder I work, the more I live. I rejoice in life for its own sake. Life is no "brief candle" to me. It is a sort of splendid torch which I have got hold of for the moment, and I want to make it burn as brightly as possible before handing it on to future generations."

"Do not let the principles presented in this book be simply information - useless without your commitment to applying them in your own life. What are the possibilities for your life? What will you do to make the most of them? What is next for you?" (George Bernard Shaw)

"Our greatest fear is not that we are inadequate. Our deepest fear is that we are powerful beyond measure. It is our light, not darkness, that most frightens us. We ask ourselves, "Who am I to be brilliant, or fabulously talented?" Actually, how dare you not? You are a being of brilliance. Your playing small doesn't serve the world.

There's nothing enlightened about shrinking so that other people won't feel insecure around you. We are all meant to shine as children do. We were born to manifest the wonderment of the gift that is within us. It's not just in some of us, it's in everyone. And as we let our light shine, we unconsciously give other people the permission to do the same. As we are liberated from our fear, our presence liberates others." (Marianne Wilson quoting Nelson Mandela)

Books, Tapes & Reports By Joe Rubino

BOOKS:

- *Secrets Of Building A Million-Dollar Network Marketing Organization From A Guy Who's Been There Done That And Shows You How To Do It, Too*
- *Principles For Powerful Living: Maximizing Your Personal Effectiveness*

TAPES:

- *Secrets Of Building A Million Dollar Network Marketing Organization: Secret 1- Self-Motivation*

Also - 21 different reports on network marketing.

All items can be ordered direct from Joe at: 978-887-3125.

Man of Distinction

It's been quite a ride for **Dr. Joe Rubino** of late. In 1995, Joe was featured on the cover of prestigious SUCCESS Magazine and in its Cover Story, "We Create Millionaires –How Network Marketing's Entrepreneurial Elite Are Building Fortunes at Breakneck Speed." His new book, "Secrets of Building a Million-Dollar Network Marketing Organization" is selling rapidly and he was recently named "1998 Man of Distinction in Network Marketing" by the International Network Marketing Directory.

Not long ago, however, network marketing wasn't even a blip on Joe Rubino's radar screen. In fact, he'd already found success in the dental practice he started in 1981. But in the early '90's he came across an ad for Oxyfresh Worldwide, a network marketing company, in a dental magazine and decided to find out more. "As I learned more and more about the potential of network marketing to impact peoples lives, I decided that I could make more of a difference by changing careers."

In 1991 he formed Visionary International Partnerships with his business partner, Dr. Tom Ventullo. Visionary International Partnerships was profitable almost immediately. Implementing Oxyfresh's products into their practice both supported their patient's health and added $4,000 plus monthly to their bottom line.

But Joe and Tom didn't stop there; they also became serious about building a network of other Oxyfresh distributors, eventually creating another income stream that increased from a few hundred dollars monthly to equal and then exceed their entire dental practice income. Soon thereafter, the dental world lost one of their own as Joe retired from practice in 1994. Dentistry's loss, however, was network marketing's gain.

"Through network marketing, I can best honor my values by developing new and innovative programs and approaches to impact peoples' success and therefore their lives." Joe admits that his attitude was shaped by some very supportive people. "Mike Smith and Carol McCall are my mentors and the ones I credit for inspiring me to take on the lifelong process of personal development, encouraging me to pursue my values while helping me see that I could have a major impact on peoples' lives.

"Mike, Carol, and Richard Brooke, CEO of Oxyfresh Worldwide, all inspired me to see that I was playing small in my profession as a dentist. They supported me in clearly identifying my values and gifts while developing a vision to design my life as one with no regrets, playing full out." ∎

The Interviews

Robert Blackman
(RB)

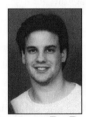

Thomas DeRosa
(TD)

Rick Eriksen
(RE)

Charles Leslie
(CL)

Joe Rubino
(JR)

GETTING STARTED:

I'm starting a home business next month. I have a maximum of $3000 in start-up capital. Where should I invest it?

JR: With $3,000 to invest I suggest spending approximately $750 on product inventory and support materials you'll need to get your business going. Spend another $750 to get fully trained, books, tapes, personal development and training seminars, etc. whatever is best recommended by your mentors, $250 to set up shop with business cards, stationery, office supplies and $1000 on a proven advertising strategy that will bring in high-quality leads in a niche you decide to target.

RE: With $3,000 I started my business by purchasing advertising co-ops to generate interested prospects.

TD: Alpine has a start-up package called the Success Pack, but the company finances it for no money down. A few hundred dollars to run some ads would suffice.

CL: 1) Select a stable, long-term network marketing company that's beginning the momentum growth stage. 2) Choose an upline with an effective support infrastructure that has the following available: co-op advertising, direct mail system, mailing services, automatic follow-up system, fax-on-demand, Web site access, welcome pack, etc. Invest in the support that fits with your marketing plan. 3) Buy basic business office supplies, business cards and letterhead. 4) Invest most of the money into a marketing plan that utilizes your time, money, and talents most effectively. The marketing plan should consist of three to four different ways to generate leads. 5) Computer and fax machine. If the business you are starting needs a fax machine and utilizes email for communication, then get them as soon as possible.

RB: A computer, a fax and a mobile head-set on your phone. I have the Office Rover. This allows me to walk & talk all day long while I have both hands free. Get a year's subscription to *Upline.* Plus, subscribe to Jay Abraham's newsletter. Then, read every book you can get your hands on about Network Marketing. I also recommend Personal Power by Tony Robbins. His tapes helped me get the right mind-set while I was in the trenches building my business.

I've just started a home business. My spouse has given me six months to make it work. Any advice?

JR: Work in partnership with your mentors who have successfully built a business and develop a detailed business plan on EXACTLY what it will take for you to succeed. Everything from the number of hours you'll spend building your business daily, weekly and monthly; to how many leaders you'll need to attract monthly; the number of people you'll need to speak with to do so; who your ideal candidate to prospect is; how many leads or prospects you'll speak with daily; where and how you'll develop your prospect list; what you'll say, send them and how and when to follow up; and what areas you'll need to become more proficient in, in order to achieve the level of success you desire. In short, first know exactly what you want to achieve, develop a detailed game plan to achieve it, expect to succeed and just do it. Oh, and don't forget to continually evaluate if your actions will produce the result you desire and fine tune it regularly.

RE: I would ask my spouse for her support in taking on the attitude that we will do whatever it takes to succeed. To persist until success comes. Six months is not enough time to make a new home business work. You must get your spouse to get behind you 100% for as long as it takes.

TD: Just set your goals and work hard towards achieving them.

CL: 1) Set goals that will keep you motivated. Do a future journaling exercise of what life will be like in six months as a result of doing this business. 2) Educate yourself about the Network Marketing Industry and how it works. 3) Realize that there is often at least a six month learning curve and it will often take at least 1-2 years to build a successful home-based network marketing business.

RB: Ask for 60! You can't really accomplish much in just your first six months. You'll spend most of that time educating yourself on your product/service and getting acquainted with being out of balance by running your own business. It took me five years to make a six-figure income. Boy, am I glad my wife gave me 60 months instead 6! Tell your spouse that your home-based business is your version of Social Security. That sheds a whole new light on your spouse's attitude towards you and your business.

They say it takes money to make money. Should I try to get a small business loan for my start-up capital or just try to get by with my own limited finances?

JR: Although I do not encourage anyone to go deeply into debt, you'll need at least a few hundred dollars to get started properly. If you are willing to work your plan and do what ever it takes to succeed, you'll easily soon be profitable. Those who prefer to get started on a shoestring can also develop a plan to succeed without a lot of money if they are willing to be creative.

RE: I do not recommend getting a small business loan. You can still make it with limited finances. I did.

TD: A small business loan is a very good idea. It's hard to get a business started from a shoe-string. I know because when I started, my wife and I were using food stamps.

CL: Cut back on any unnecessary personal spending and invest that money into the business. Sell any items that you no longer need. Start a separate checking account to feed money into the business. Initially, put all of the money you earn back into the business. Only at last resort would I recommend getting a small business loan.

RB: I went bankrupt with loans. Getting a loan made it easy for me to take stupid risks. Without my loans I would of gotten back to work and stopped all those crazy deals I just knew were going make me rich. It wasn't until I focused on one way of making money and committed to a consistent pattern did I ever start making large amounts of money.

Do you consider yourself an "early adopter" of new technology?

JR: I consider myself to be a paradigm pioneer, someone willing to anticipate the future and act with courage and foresight. This can mean adopting early technology if it appears to be promising.

RE: Yes.

TD: I love technology! I've been technologically-oriented for many years.

CL: No.

RB: No. I'm a latecomer to technology. But, I couldn't live without my computer, fax machine and cell phone.

Describe your computer(s) and peripherals used:

JR: PC, Microsoft Office. 37. We also use a scanner and color printer.

RE: IBM compatible, 486 Intel processor, 32 mb ram, 1 Gig hard drive. Microsoft Windows 95, Laser Jet III printer.

TD: Power Macintosh, Umax scanner, digital camera, Cannon printer, Global Village 56k modems

CL: Gateway 2000.

RB: Four IBM's and one Mac. Also, a color scanner and Zip drive, three printers.

What software do you consider in the "must-have" category?

JR: Windows 95, Word, Internet Explorer, An email program, Quick View (to open incompatible files).

RE: Microsoft Publisher for desktop publishing, ACT for contact management, Quicken for personal finances.

TD: ClarisWorks.

CL: Microsoft Windows; ACT contact management - this has made mailings to my downline and prospects much more professional and time-efficient;

Technology Utilized

	Fax*	Fax-on-Demand	Toll-Free	Voice Mail	Computer	Email	Internet	Email Auto-Responders
Joe Rubino	✓	✓	✓	✓	✓	✓	✓	✓
Rick Eriksen	✓	✓	✓	✓	✓	✓	✓	
Thomas DeRosa	✓	✓	✓	✓	✓	✓	✓	✓
Charles Leslie	✓	✓	✓	✓	✓	✓	✓	✓
Robert Blackman	✓	✓	✓	✓	✓	✓	✓	✓

* Dedicated fax line

Quickbooks PRO - this has made it much easier to verify how our company is doing financially, at any time of the year, and any time of the month. Profit and Loss statements as well as expenses can be printed quickly. It has made tax time far less of a headache.

RB: Microsoft Word & PageMaker

What is the primary use for your toll-free line?

JR: Advertising. We do massive advertising and have about 40 toll-free number extensions.

RE: My primary use for my 800 line is in certain promotional material.

TD: Advertising responses.

CL: For advertising responses.

RB: Credit card orders for my books and tapes.

What other technologies, if any, do you use in your business?

JR: Cellular phones, laptop computers.

RE: No other techno tools. I cancelled my cell phone and pager for lack of use. I work at home and rarely use these tools.

TD: Cell phone, Power Macintosh laptop computer.

CL: Headset "hands free" phone - a must for people like me who are on the phone all of the time.

RB: Portable Headset, Cell Phone, Laptop computer, Portable hand scanner

Of all the technology you use, rank the top three:

JR: Voice mail, email, 3-way calling.

RE: Computer, my printer, my fax machine.

TD: Phone, computer, e-mail.

CL: Voice mail, fax, computer.

RB: Computer, fax machine, portable headset.

Do you market on the Internet?

JR: Yes, by sending people to our sites with traditional and online ads and offers for free subscriptions to our newsletters.

RE: Yes, I market on the internet with respect to the Web sites available from my company TPN and my upline.

TD: Yes, I direct people to my Web site through direct mail and personal contacts.

CL: Yes, in co-op advertising.

RB: Yes, with www.networkmarketing.com

Approximately what % of your sales originate from Internet marketing?
JR: 10%

RE: Zero

TD: My website just helps to reinforce my presentation. Alpine is unable to effectively monitor income and product claims that independent reps sometimes make, so they don't approve of internet advertising. The company that I will start with my income from Alpine will be on the internet.

CL: I have done very little to date, no statistics available.

RB: 2%

Do you use direct mail?
JR: Yes, ads for our opportunity. Also postcards and letters targeting our exact markets.

RE: Yes. By sending postcards to generate interested prospects, but mostly with follow-up letters professionally printed and personalized.

TD: Yes. Self-contained mailing brochures, postcards.

CL: Yes, I use postcards.

RB: I mail directly to rented lists and four times a year to my customers.

Approximately what % of your sales originate from direct mail marketing?
JR: 10%

RE: 100% of my sales come from my follow-up letters.

TD: About 15%.

CL: 10%

Do you use print media?
JR: Yes, extensive advertising campaigns in magazines (Business, health, professional, and general interest), newspapers, card decks and professional journals and newsletters.

RE: Yes, by plugging into advertising co-ops sponsored by my immediate upline.

TD: Yes, magazines and newspapers, classified and display ads.

CL: Yes, magazines, newspapers, card decks.

RB: Yes, I run ads in magazines, card decks, and newspapers.

Approximately what % of your sales originate from print media marketing?
JR: 60%
RE: 90% of my interested prospects come from advertising co-ops that primarily use print media.
TD: About 65%.
CL: 75%
RB: 95%

Do you use radio and/or TV advertising?
JR: We use radio ad campaigns at target markets, accounting for about 5% of our total sales.
RE: No.
TD: Not currently.
CL: No.
RB: Not yet.

What other kinds of marketing do you utilize?
JR: Trade, health and professional shows represented by booths.
RE: No other kinds of marketing have worked for me.
TD: Mostly trade shows, some cold calling, a fair amount of person-to-person contacts.
CL: Fairs & shows, flyers.
RB: Warm marketing. I am always exchanging business cards and leaving "take one" stands wherever I can. Plus, I still network with the Chamber, etc.

Do you recommend using a toll-free number in advertising? Why or why not?
JR: Yes, whenever advertising beyond a local area. By increasing the prospect's convenience, you increase the number of leads generated.
RE: Yes, I recommend toll-free numbers in marketing because more people will respond and it adds credibility.
TD: Yes, it adds credibility.
CL: Yes. Research reveals that people are more likely to respond to a toll-free number.
RB: Only if you're sure you can handle the costs. I've been running ads for 10 years now and I know exactly what to expect when I put an 800# in a card deck going to 200,000 people, do you? I used to take the fish-net approach when I first started. I just threw out my net and I'd pull everything I caught in my boat - including the sharks! But, today, I find that I only want to work personally with those who are qualified. I qualify them by selling a book or tape first, and then I work with them. It's kind of like going through your catch first, before you bring everything into your boat.

Where do you market?

JR: Locally, nationally, internationally.

RE: I market primarily in the USA but also Canada. In the future I plan to go worldwide.

TD: Locally and nationally.

CL: Throughout North America using a variety of advertising methods. In 1998 my marketing plan is focused on the Pacific Northwest and promoting local seminars.

RB: Local and nationally.

How should someone set up their home office to maximize its effectiveness?

JR: Home office should be set up efficiently with privacy, quiet and convenience in mind. Easily accessible materials, tools, and all other items needed.

RE: A separate room is best, but my bedroom doubles as my office and it works fine. (I am also single and live alone).

TD: Most importantly, it should be well-removed from the rest of the house. A large work area is necessary to keep organized. Surround yourself with your goals and motivations. A computer and fax machine are vital, files and literature organizers help tremendously.

CL: 1) Color-code and organize by divisions - about a year ago I implemented the "Rainbows of Joy" system created by Joy Gilfilen which includes organizing the office files, binders, and notebooks by color according to divisions: Executive Director; Financial & Legal; Information & Communications; Development; Marketing & Planning; Public Relations; Activities; Quality Control. 2) Dedicate a room to be used for office space. 3) Dedicated business phone/fax/modem.

RB: Keep the room separate from the rest of the house. I put motivational posters, awards, letters from satisfied customers and a stereo in my home office. Plus, you need a WINDOW! I love looking outside watching my daughter play while I'm taking an order over the phone!

Are there any ground rules you've established for yourself, family, etc. for operating at home successfully?

JR: A request is made for privacy without non-emergency interruption whenever a "do not disturb" sign is evident.

RE: No ground rules until my future wife moves in with me.

TD: Yes, "I love you guys, but keep out of my office while I'm working!"

CL: I answer my phone and my wife answers her phone. We don't pick up each other's phone unless the other requests it. This way no messages are lost or misunderstood. We remind ourselves often that we are a corporation with different divisions and roles and that it is important to act professionally.

RB: Keep the hours set, if possible. Let your spouse and kids know that when you hit that room you mean business. Put a small refrigerator in your office. This will keep you from making 50 trips a day procrastinating. When you go in your office go to work. When you leave your office reward yourself for your hard work - then you'll look forward to going back in there.

Do you consider working at home an advantage or disadvantage to your business overall?

JR: A huge advantage. It's inexpensive, comfortable and convenient.

RE: For me working at home is a huge advantage. It gives me the freedom to start at 4AM if I want and to work till late at night if I want.

TD: A major advantage in terms of spending time with my family. Also, since there is no commute, I can devote even more time to running my business, and can do so at will.

CL: Because this is a people-to-people business I meet people at their homes and offices or talk to them over the telephone. About 90% of my work has been done on the telephone, so I find working at home to be much less stressful, more comfortable, and best of all - only a thirty second commute!

RB: I have both a home office and an office at my printing plant. My home office has less distractions and I'm able to write and personally recruit more productively. The only problem with a home office is that if you're not careful you'll have the miserable feeling that you're always at work! Set ground rules. Go in at 10 and come out at 2. Then go back in at 6 and work until 8. That way, having your office at home doesn't become a big negative.

Do you farm out any of your work?

JR: We delegate responsibilities when appropriate, always with an eye to be efficient, effective and empowering. Various tasks from creating different elements of new projects to lead distribution to advertising set-up.

RE: Yes, I farm out graphic design, printing, copies.

TD: No.

CL: In the past we created support services that consumed all of our time by creating co-op advertising efforts, mailing services, and other support services. Our upline has a built-in system of support with full-time secretaries and professional support that frees us up to do the critical actions of recruiting.

RB: Yes, some of my books and tapes are done with outside sources - along with an answering service to take calls after hours.

Do you encourage or discourage partnerships? How about hiring family members?

JR: Highly ENCOURAGE partnershipping. Our name says it all–Visionary International PARTNERSHIPS. We encourage effective relationships and partnering together with others. Hiring family members depends on the individual; if the members have the necessary skills, a good attitude and are willing to be open to coaching and feedback, it can work well. If the willingness to do whatever it takes to make it work is lacking, I would not.

RE: I discourage partnerships for network marketing. The start-up costs are way too small to complicate a distributorship with a partner. Yes, I encourage hiring family members.

TD: Encourage only for those rare relationships between people that are synergistic. Hiring family members? I don't personally feel it is a good idea, because your judgment with business decisions that involve family members can become compromised.

RB: After working 10 years with my wife and family, I would have to say if you're going to work together you had better understand each other's strengths and weaknesses beforehand. Have a set job that each of you do. Don't crossover too much. Working with my wife was both rewarding and unrewarding. The rewarding is priceless. The unrewarding can be prevented - even if you have to seek counseling or go to a workshop - do it. It will open the lines of communication and proper expectations for each of you.

When legal issues arise, what's your usual response?

JR: We always look for a win-win scenario with an intent to listen for other people's concerns and commitments, doing the right thing and honoring others.

RE: When legal issues arise I depend on my company's legal staff. I see no need to hire my own attorneys.

TD: Call a lawyer – that's their area of expertise, not mine.

CL: Investigate to find the information they want, and take the actions to solve it.

RB: Get a good attorney and great CPA. I've been sued twice and been audited twice. There's nothing more frustrating than to have all your hard work go down the drain because you don't have good counsel. It's not cheap either - but, hey, neither is your freedom!

MONEY & INVESTMENTS:

Does earning a lot of money improve the quality of your life, and if so, in what ways?

JR: Money is an amplifier of intentions. It in itself is neither good nor evil. It can certainly be used for much good. It does improve quality of life for all involved. When you don't have to worry about having enough money, you can focus on doing what's most important to you, including contributing to others and living your values, vision and life purpose.

RE: Yes, absolutely. Money improves the quality of my life. If there was no money there would be no freedom to do what I want to do, with whom I want to do it with and when I want to do it.

TD: Yes! My family and I travel about every other month, and Alpine pays the bill! We love to travel. We eat out whenever we want (quite often), purchase whatever we need, and have money to invest in our health and well-being. I have two new luxury cars as opposed to a broken-down jeep that I had just two years ago. Also, earning a six-figure income gives me a small sense of accomplishment, so I feel better about myself overall. And lastly, with many financial pressures removed, I feel that there is much less stress on myself and my family.

CL: Money, when handled in the proper way, can enrich your life and provide you with the means to make your dreams come true. For me, earning a six-figure income has allowed me to: 1) Be more joyful and enjoy eating quality organic foods that enrich my health and enhance my vitality without having to worry about the grocery bill. 2) Take numerous vacations, without going into debt - vacations that have greatly enriched my relationship with my wife and family. 3) Invest my profits and watch them grow.

RB: Yes. First of all, it allowed my wife to stop working at my office and have our daughter. We had worked for 10 years together before we could afford to allow her to quit work. Secondly, she was irreplaceable. Nobody, and I mean nobody has or ever will do as good as job as she did. When she quit, I had to totally restructure my business. It hurt. But, because we were making a 6-figure income we could afford to restructure properly without going crazy. Plus, having extra money allows us to do nice things for our friends and family members. Travel is another example. My wife and I love to stay at the Broadmoor in Colorado Springs. Golf, massages, a trip to Pikes Peak - and the food is incredible! After a week at the Broadmoor you'll not only realize the reason why you're in your own business, but you'll also need to be - it's expensive!

Best general tax advice?

JR: Create a successful network marketing business and legitimately write off your lifestyle.

RE: Always pay your taxes and always file your returns.

TD: Write off everything that's a possibility, save your receipts, and hire a great accountant!

CL: Keep track of all expenses. Utilize a software program. Analyze your profit and loss statement monthly. Get a good tax accountant. Make sure to listen to David D'Archangelo's *"Strike It Rich"* Program. He has over 49 tax advantages for the home-based entrepreneur.

RB: Ask your CPA. By the way, get two of them. Have the first one do your taxes and then have your second one proof the first. Also, get educated. Don't allow your apparent wealth to go to your head. Making money means responsibility. If you're not careful, making lots of money can make you lazy! So, be prepared.

Best general investment advice?

JR: If you've got it made, it's neither wise nor necessary to foolishly risk it. Invest wisely considering your risk tolerance, years until retirement and objectives.

RE: Caveat Emptor: Buyer Beware. Be extremely careful where you put your money. Only do business with people who were referred to you by trusted friends or family. Investment ripoffs are rampant and scrutinize every investment very carefully. Do NOT take on high risk gambles.

TD: Heavily research your investments, and monitor them as well.

CL: Best general investment advice? Find a good financial advisor that does not charge high commissions and makes all of his/her money when your money grows. Build a diversified portfolio.

RB: The same as my advice on taxes.

You're in business already, and you've just received a windfall of $20,000. What would you do with it?

JR: Invest the $20,000 where it will produce the greatest return. Ask yourself, what is missing to take your business to the next level and spend it there.

RE: I would put $15,000 in advertising co-ops and $5,000 in follow-up letters. In my business, there will never be a better return than generating interested prospects and doing repeated follow-up.

TD: Buy additional stock in Oracle, and use some of the money to advertise. In other words, reinvest in my business. I can spend more money later.

CL: Tithe...10% ($2,000), save in liquid funds...20% ($4,000), invest with financial advisor...50% ($10,000), invest in marketing plan strategies...20% ($4,000).

RB: Take $5,000 of it and re-invest it back into your business with ads, letters or training for you, your employees or your downline. Take another $5,000 and put it away into your best tax-free investment. Take another 5,000 and give it to your spouse and say "have fun, hun!" With the last $5,000 I'd spend it on myself! Look, the reason I got into my own business is to write my own paycheck. Sure, some would re-invest the entire $20,000 into their business - that's an option. But, after working for myself for over 11 years now I have found that unless YOU reward yourself nobody else will. And burn-out or depression WILL occur if you simply just WORK, WORK, WORK. Learn how to have some fun along the way. Buy or do something totally selfish with your $5,000. Because when you do, then you'll realize that your reason WHY is fueled more and more.

What do you lead with–your company's products or the business opportunity?

JR: The opportunity most of the time –unless you specifically can identify a clear product need. And even then, offer the business opportunity along with it in a way that they can "get it." If you want to attract product users, lead with the products. If you want to attract entrepreneurs, as we do, lead with the opportunity. We also prefer to advertise the opportunity- not product.

RE: I always lead with the business opportunity. Big Time income comes from simple & easy DUPLICATION of advertising and that only comes from people who have a desire for financial freedom from a home-business opportunity.

TD: I don't mean to be vague, but both. Different circumstances require different approaches. Our exclusive air and water purification technologies are far removed from the typical pills, potions, phones and lotion products. I believe that our product goes hand in hand with our opportunity.

CL: I usually lead with the business opportunity, but on occasion I will mention the products first. It depends on the situation and which product I may want to promote to the individual.

RB: I run ads for both techniques. I believe that if you're committed, you could build your Network Marketing business either way - product or business opportunity. But, if I would have to do it all over again, I would focus more on retailing and the products first. The reason why is over 50% of those in your downline will NEVER make a commission check - those are the cold hard facts. So, in 90 days when they got into your program to make money and they're not, they go looking for something else. They have to, they still have a money problem. But, when you lead with the product that they love and enjoy, they'll buy it from you or your company REGARDLESS if they are making any money or not. Case in point. I have one company where I am still making around $1,500 a month with them. Yet, I haven't put one person in the program, or talked to one downline member for over 4 years! They're all product-users!

Rank the following traits in order of their importance in building a success-ful network marketing business: enthusiasm, persistence, knowledge, communication skills.

JR: Communication skills, enthusiasm, persistence, knowledge

RE: Persistence, enthusiasm, knowledge, communication skills

TD: Persistence, communication skills, enthusiasm, knowledge. I put knowledge last because I had no prior MLM experience, and also because all of the knowledge in the world is useless when it is not applied.

CL: Persistence, enthusiasm, communication skills, knowledge.

RB: Enthusiasm, persistence, communication skills, knowledge.

How long were you in network marketing before you saw your first four-fig-ure commission check? Five-figure check?

JR: With our product outlet, we reached a four-figure check in our second month. It took about 12 months to see our first five-figure check.

RE: My first four-figure income check took 6 months. My first five-figure income check took 9 months.

TD: $1,100 my third month; $7,400 check in 6th month. 11th month; just over $10,200.

CL: Five months for the former, 3 1/2 years for the latter.

RB: 2 years, 5 years

What's more important –the initial contact with a prospect or the follow-up?

JR: Both are equally important in that you need to initially contact someone in a timely and powerful manner and also follow-up the same way. The gold lies in the follow-up which is most often neglected.

RE: Repeated follow-up is the most important.

TD: First impressions are more important, but the follow-up is an intricate part of the overall recruiting process.

CL: The follow-up.

RB: Initial contact. You have only one chance at a good first impression. If you make a lousy first impression it doesn't matter how great your follow-up is-if they don't like you, they won't do business with you.

You've just recruited a promising new distributor – how do you help them get off to a good start –or do you consider that the new distributor's responsibili-ty?

JR: It's a shared responsibility. As the sponsor it's your responsibility to get the new distributor trained and set up in a duplicable, detailed and effective manner. A simple and duplicable system which includes a detailed game plan is a must. That's your responsibility as a sponsor. The new distributor's responsibility is to be open to training and to stay coachable.

RE: I make sure they have my welcome letter as well as my upline's Welcome Package. I make sure my new distributor understands that the THREE RITUALS OF SUCCESS are generating interested prospects through advertising co-ops or postcards, sending 7 professionally printed follow-up letters over 7-14 weeks, and making phone calls and sending newsletters to those that prove their interests by investing about $20 for our premium information package.

TD: It is my responsibility to give that new distributor the tools and training that they need. I help them get off to a good start by teaching them the importance of GOALSETTING. I can't help those who won't help themselves! Much of the "how to" is contained in a Welcome Newsletter that I send to all new Distributors. Then, 3-way calls are a great way to start training that new Distributor.

CL: I definitely help them get off to a good start by developing a firm foundation of how the business works and the products that the company has available. From me they will learn about the variety of resources they have available. I also help them create a marketing plan and make three-way calls with them for the first month.

RB: I always ask them what their top three reasons for getting into the business are. Then, I ask them what specific dollar amount they are wanting to earn. Then I map-out a specific game plan. This includes dollar amount they need to spend every month, how many people they need to sponsor, how to understand the pay plan, the products, etc.

In five years I'll be....

JR: ...continuing to live my vision of being an internationally known force inspiring others to kill the resignation in their lives by knowing that they can be, do, and have anything they desire if they can envision it, believe and expect it and set out with a clear and specific plan to achieve it. My books will be responsible for contributing to the lives of at least one million people. I will be recognized as a leader in the world in network marketing and for championing people to be all they can be. My network marketing organization will comprise 1,000,000 successful friends and partners.

RE: In five years I'll be earning in excess of $100,000 per month making a positive difference in people lives.

TD: In five years I'll be 28, and the owner of a multi-million-dollar internet-related company with my business partner, Todd Kleperis.

CL: I'll be...35 and a millionaire in full-time pursuit of my non-profit endeavors and spending full-time in voluntary ministry.

RB: In five years I'll have my own info-mercial selling my books, tapes and MLM Mastery Course.

In ten years I'll be...

JR: In ten years, due to our efforts in partnering with other network marketing leaders, the world will view network marketing as the most effective means of contributing to the financial and personal freedom of others. We will have shifted the paradigm that people must work at jobs they do not love for 40+ years only to retire on less than they could afford to comfortably live on while working. People will finally realize that they can direct their lives and their futures if they have the courageous expectation that they can.

RE: In ten years I'll be earning in excess of $500,000 per month making a positive difference in many more peoples lives all over North America.

TD: I'll be 33, and the owner of a 500 million dollar publicly-traded company.

RB: In ten years I'll have 50,000 people in my organization and I'll only work in-depth by giving meetings and speaking at conventions.

What most motivates you in building your business?

JR: My vision as noted earlier is to impact people's lives and to shift from paradigms that do not support their greatness.

RE: What most motivates me in building my business is the fear of working for some incompetent bozo and losing my freedom to do what I want, when I want, with whomever I want.

TD: Money, although that motivating factor should not be equated with greed. Money enables me to acquire other more important things, such as a home for my family and an education for my daughter.

CL: In the beginning it was the desire to be debt-free, to break the chains and the burden of debt. Now it is time, freedom, the opportunity to pursue my true passion and purpose, and to create a financial base so that I can live off of my investments.

RB: My time. The freedom to do what I want, when I want it.

How often do you read books and/or listen to or watch tapes for improving your business skills or knowledge?

JR: Almost daily.

RE: I watch or read or listen to personal development tapes, books and programs on a daily basis: about 30-60 minutes each day. It's a lot easier to do this with the SUCCESS CHANNEL .

TD: About 1 hour per day.

CL: I watch The Peoples Network's Success Channel daily. I also read the network marketing industry trade and watchdog magazines.

RB: Every single day. I read in the morning and evening and listen during the day. You eat food everyday to keep alive, don't you? Then, why don't you feed your mind three times a day for your emotional and spiritual well-being? Nobody, and I mean nobody, can run a successful business without some type of daily self-improvement program - it's essential

Editor's Note: The Success Channel is the new 24-hour television network devoted exclusively to positive, personal development programming. For more information, contact your World Team Contact Person.

The most underrated activity in business is?

JR: Looking to generate new possibilities that help more people to win.

RE: The most underrated activity in business is personal development. Here is where dreams and desires are ignited.

TD: Sleep! It's the cornerstone of concentration and human performance.

CL: Follow-up.

RB: Investing your time and energy into your customers and downline members

The most overrated activity in business is?

JR: Getting others to do something because it serves you.

RE: The most overrated business activity is talking to friends and family about a business opportunity. I've never met anyone in my life who was successful doing this in network marketing.

TD: The most overrated activity in business is lunch.

RB: Recruiting. So much time is spent on recruiting and very little time is spent on customer acquisition and creating a system to where anyone can do what you do.

If you had to start your business all over again, what would you do differently?

JR: Develop a clear vision of what I was playing for, what was at stake in terms of my life, vitality and potential contribution to others and a resulting game plan to achieve this vision from the start.

RE: I would have doubled or tripled my advertising co-op investments.

Generating interested prospects starts the process. The more interested prospects who enter the pipeline the better.

TD: I would have started out much earlier.

CL: I would be a firm leader, one who worked with people, not for people. I would also focus on attracting people to my business rather than convincing or recruiting them to join my team.

RB: I would retail more and I would also read *How To Win Friends & Influence People* once a month. Learning how to deal with people and network is what has made my business so successful.

What was your worst business decision?

JR: To play small, not go for the brass ring so to speak in the beginning out of lacking the belief in myself and the impact our industry can have on people's lives.

RE: My worst business decision in the past was promoting more than one network marketing company. All you end up doing is losing credibility with people.

TD: Due to my lack of network marketing experience, I had just about quit even though I was already earning over $7,000 per month. I had to cope with the fact that some people will fail regardless of my help. I can't help those who won't help themselves, and those who can't follow directions.

RB: Trusting a business partner completely and hanging on their every word. It came back to haunt me.

What was your best business decision?

JR: To enter into a commitment to lifelong personal development work for myself and others.

RE: My best decision is joining The Peoples Network, but especially within the Gery Carson Six-Figure Income Marketing Group. The advertising and marketing tools available from Gery are a network marketer's dream!!!

TD: The conscious decision that I was going to achieve the goals that I set.

CL: Getting involved with Gery Carson's Six-Figure Income Marketing Group. His organization provides the professional and efficient support my downline and I can utilize to build a large successful business without the burden of creating our own support services.

RB: To get involved in Network Marketing. When my printing business failed in 1990 I could have quit and gotten a job. But, I didn't. Instead, I found another printing company that was going out of business and with no money down, made the monthly bank payments. But, what turned me around was that I got involved in Network Marketing while I was also running my own printing business. Today, they work hand-in-hand!

What do you consider to be the main keys of your success?

JR: A clear and compelling vision for my life and what is possible. A detailed plan to make it happen. A commitment to make decisions daily that support my vision as opposed to decisions of convenience.

RE: The main keys to my success is my persistence: I will never, ever, ever, ever, give up....period.

TD: Goalsetting, persistence, and hard work.

CL: 1) Persistence - I remember that when I got involved with network marketing there were a couple of other people that got started at the same time that I did. They had much more talent and were more effective in the beginning, but they have since dropped out and I have stuck with it. My success has come from sticking with it and following the basics. *"Nothing can take the place of persistence... talent will not, the world is full of unrewarded men with talent, genius will not, unrewarded genius is almost a proverb - persistence and determination alone."* 2) Belief –I always believe that what I set my mind to do I can achieve. 3) Give myself no option to fail. 4) Good mentorship and support. 5) God is my strength.

RB: Helping others first. When my downline succeeds, then I succeed.

What's your success philosophy?

JR: Most anyone can succeed if they have a clear and empowering vision that motivates them to re-invent themselves to be maximally effective in their listening and communication skills with others and the courage to develop and pursue an action plan to get there. Also, by identifying one's most important values and honoring them it is possible to live a life of no regrets that can be designed on purpose.

RE: My SUCCESS philosophy: WHATEVER IT TAKES!!!

TD: I believe that in order to become successful, one must first have a strong desire to succeed, and should set out to pursue something that they love.

CL: I set out a vision, goals, and marketing plan for my business. To internalize all of this, I create a future journaling audio tape in which I speak of what it feels like to have accomplished these goals. I listen to this daily until my goals are accomplished.

RB: If you change other people's lives, then your life will automatically be fulfilled.

What about you has changed the most since finding success in business?

JR: With success has come the opportunity to devote more time and energy to personal development and to supporting others to realize their greatness.

RE: The thing that has changed the most since finding success in business is FREEDOM. Freedom from incompetent bozo bosses, freedom to go sailing, skiing, or golfing whenever I want, and the freedom to help those in need and the rewards of knowing that I make a positive difference in the lives of other people.

TD: My ability to set goals and achieve them, and my knowledge of people in general.

CL: Confidence in who I am and what I can still accomplish.

RB: My patience. I was very impatient at first. So impatient that I got into every type of business opportunity and Network Marketing deal that came around - thinking that the ideal held the answer I was looking for. Not so. The answer was in me. I had to find and develop a belief system that I would and could take to my grave with me. Then, and only then, did I find the strength to stick with one program and work it.

What is the legacy you hope to leave?

JR: To have left the world a better place in which others are more clear of their ability to impact change for the better. To help others realize that each of us possesses the seeds of greatness if we can become personally free to pursue our dreams, values and contribute our gift to the world. I also seek to kill the living death that resignation brings to people's lives. To inspire people to believe in themselves and others and to have the courage to live their dreams.

RE: The legacy I hope to leave is that Rick Eriksen was a man of integrity, a man totally committed to his wife and family, and a man that has an attitude of doing whatever it takes to make a positive difference in the lives of everyone he touches.

TD: Like that of my hero, Larry Ellison. To forge a dominant technology company. Also, to have raised my daughter Hailey so that she, too, can set out to achieve whatever goals she will set for herself.

CL: When people think of me and the work I have accomplished here on earth, I want them to think of a shining lighthouse. I want to be considered as someone who lit the path of hope and possibility. A quote on giving from a plaque I have in my office with a shining lighthouse says it well, "One of life's greatest rules...'You cannot hold a torch to light another's path without brightening your own.'"

RB: That my children don't have to go through all the heartache that I have had to. You see, although my parents were great people, they weren't FREE. So, they only taught me what they knew - hard work. Well, hard work isn't the only ingredient to success. I wish I would have had the insight to walk away from a few business deals that I thought I could fix with hard work - and they eventually bankrupted me. I want my friends and family to learn from me that doing what you love is where the true satisfaction of life comes from. I want all my friends and family to never have to worry about another credit card or bank payment ever again. Instead, I want them to find their freedom and satisfaction in their own business - whatever that may be.

Brian Biro

Age: 43

Family: "Incredible" wife Carole, 47, and "two beautiful daughters:" Kelsey, age 11 and Jenna, age 6.

Highest Education: MBA from UCLA. Undergraduate degree is from Stanford.

Year started business: 1993

Type of business: Professional speaker, seminar teacher, and author.

Market: Large, medium, and small corporations, associations, network marketing organizations, government organizations, teachers, parents, and students.

Number of employees: One

Best month (gross revenues): $112,000

Hours worked per week during start-up: Around 40-50

Hours worked per week now: about 40

Favorite business magazines: *Personal Excellence, Executive Excellence*

Favorite business books and authors: *7 Habits of Highly Effective People, Leadership is an Art.*

Relaxes by: Exercise, reading, playing with his children, massage.

Keeps in shape physically by: Playing racquetball and running.

Favorite part of business: "I love so much of my work. First, I feel I am doing what I was put on the planet to do when I speak and teach. I LOVE and BELIEVE in people. I truly enjoy coaching and helping others bring out their genius. The opportunity to help others choose more love than fear in their lives - the breakthrough – WOW! I love the fact that my work extends beyond work and profession into home and family. In my writing I absolutely revel in the opportunity to create and to crystalize thoughts that can assist people in finding new possibilities in their lives, greater inspiration, and deeper compassion. I LOVE WHAT I DO!"

Least favorite part of business: Collections.

Companies admired: Moments By Mail is a young growing company with a mission and basic idea he truly admires. He feels they are in the business of helping companies and individuals CONNECT in a very genuine, impacting, and positive way. He has also enjoyed his work with several wonderful network marketing companies because the people are so "alive, open, and hungry to grow."

Favorite quotes:

"The love we fail to share is the only pain we live with." *(Brian Biro)*

"It's what you learn after you know everything that makes the difference!" *(John Wooden)*

"It's not just what we DO that makes the difference — it's the love we put into the doing!" *(Mother Teresa)*

Family is First with Brian Biro

BY JAN WALLEN

Brian Biro is definitely a family man. He says his wife Carole and their children have had the greatest, most meaningful influence on his life. He wanted to create a livelihood that allowed him to be with his family much more than when he was in the corporate arena. He also wanted to be able to choose where they live." I wanted to work in my home – away from traffic and to be able to generate the income we wanted without having to live the story of the powerful classic song, 'The Cat's in the Cradle.' I was determined to create a joyful, abundant livelihood while finding great balance."

And, indeed, Brian has achieved that and more. After taking the plunge into working for himself in network marketing, Brian reached a profit during the first month. And he has never looked back. He wrote a best seller, *Beyond Success*, and he has appeared on Good Morning America, CNN's Business Unusual, and the Fox News Network. He was also rated the number one speaker from over 50 nationally certified speakers at each of the last two INC Magazine National Customer Service programs.

In addition to his family, he has three heroes. The first is Coach Jim Wooden. "Coach Wooden is a shining example of humility, living one's principles and peace of mind. He is the greatest of all time in his profession, yet never seeks credit or plaudits. He lives one of his favorite quotes: 'It's amazing what gets accomplished when no one cares who gets the credit.'"

Brian has studied Mahatma Gandhi extensively and continually marvels at his amazing dedication to learning. "He never stopped growing and searching for more truth. His unshakable belief in peace, compassion, and human dignity changed the world for the better."

Mother Teresa has also provided a great deal of inspiration for Brian. "I wept when we lost Mother Teresa last summer. She was the most beautiful example of service I have ever seen. She taught us that service is love in action. Ultimately, despite living virtually all of her life in the midst of abject poverty and pain, she shined with joy. There is nothing more magnificent than true giving, and Mother Teresa lived every moment with that spirit."

Brian finds it difficult to stop talking about his family. "Every single day they give me unstoppable inspiration. Every single day they fill my heart with purpose. And every single day they remind me of what is truly important."As he reflects on his reasons for embarking into network marketing, Brian concludes, "The final key was the passion and sense of fulfilling my purpose I feel when I teach, speak, and write. Everyday I feel grateful for the freedom I feel in my life. YESSS! Life is GOOD!"

And indeed, Brian Biro has made a good life for himself and his family thanks to the opportunities present in the industry of network marketing. ■

Marty Challenger

Age: 54

Family: Married 20+ years to wife, Carol. The couple have three children: a 19-year-old daughter (Vicki), a 17-year-old daughter (Kristi), and a 15-year-old son (Jason).

Highest Education: 2 years of college.

Employees: None.

Year started business: Started his first business at age 19 in 1963.

Type of Business: Seminar speaker providing income opportunity seminars for self-employed entrepreneurs home based professionals. Specifically, Marty teaches others how to present $5,000 cruise vacation packages for only $1295, and profit $1,000 from each package. His training program teaches proven methods for averaging 1 to 2 sales everyday... working from home with nothing more than a telephone.

Best month (gross revenue): 53 sales, which translates to $53,000.

Hours worked per week during start-up: 30

Hours worked per week now: 35-40

Favorite Business Magazines: *Success, Working at Home, Six-Figure Income.*

Favorite Business Books/Authors: Anthony Robbins, Zig Ziglar, Les Brown.

Relaxes by: Reading, walking on the beach.

Favorite part of his business: Talking to new friends on the telephone.

Least favorite part of his business: Not being able to reach those who do not believe in themselves.

Stays in shape by: 10 mile/day hiking, recumbent bike riding.

Admired Companies: The Peoples Network, Carson Services Inc., Cutting Edge Media.

Marty Challenger Gains Independence Through Self-Employment

BY JAN WALLEN

Marty Challenger lives up to his name. He is a self-described rebel, who wants independence and no boss hanging over him telling him what to do. He had his first job at age 19 where someone told him what to do, when to do it, how to do it, and then watched over him all day while he did it. That was a valuable learning experience as he made the decision that no matter what he did for a living, he would be independent.

Today he has achieved that goal several times over. He began with a carpet and upholstery cleaning service, then had a rain gutter repair and installation service, a full scale building contractor business and a guard and patrol service. Presently he is involved in network marketing and is teaching others how to do what he has done.

Marty says the person who most influenced his life was Anthony Robbins; he also considers Brian Tracy, Zig Ziglar and Les Brown to be valuable mentors.

When Marty began his network marketing business, he was profitable within the first month. Today he speaks on radio and TV talk shows, telling others how to achieve the same success, by using his "fast-start, smart-start" home-based program. The network marketing industry allows anyone to profit substantially.

Marty enjoys all the benefits of being his own boss. He says, "The best thing about being self-employed is definitely the freedom of choice and the freedom of movement. I wouldn't trade it for anything!"

We live in a country where the American dream can still come true for people like Marty Challenger. ■

Tracy Dieterich

Age: 33

Family: single.

Highest Education: B.S. from College of Engineering at Texas A&M University.

Year started business: April, 1993.

Type of business: Network marketing – recently he has added a seminar business and vending machine business.

Market: Motivated and teachable individuals who want to develop residual income for life.

Number of employees: One part-timer.

Best month (gross revenues): $35,878

Hours worked per week during start-up: 80+

Hours worked per week now: 10-12

Favorite business magazines: *Success, Robb Report, Money.*

Favorite business books and authors: Og Mandino is his favorite author and he loves all his books – his favorite: *The Spellbinder's Gift*. He also likes *The Richest Man in Babylon* by Classen and the best-selling book of all time – The Bible.

Relaxes by: Vacationing, exercising, reading and sunbathing.

Keeps in shape by: Lifts weights and uses the treadmill 2-3 times per week. Also, plays racquetball 1-2 times a month.

Favorite part of job: Speaking to a great audience.

Least favorite part of job: Watching people who have ability (and needs) fail because they lack desire.

Companies admired: Microsoft, Dell Computer, Amway – the pioneer.

Favorite Quotes:

"Everything changes when you change" (Jim Rohn)

"You become what you think about" (Earl Nightengale)

"You can get everything you want if you help enough others get what they want" (Zig Ziglar)

Tracy Dieterich takes in the latest issue of Six-Figure Magazine before taking off

Tracy Dieterich Proves It's Possible to Achieve Dreams

BY JAN WALLEN

It was a college friend who first invited Tracy Dieterich to take a look at a network marketing company. And he has never looked back.

Tracy had a dream - a dream of becoming his own boss. And he has been able to live that dream through network marketing. His dream was so big that when he first started in his new business, he reached the top level in the company in NINE days - a record that still stands today. Out of over 100,000 distributors, he also was one of only 25 people who reached the top level.

Tracy says that while he has had many mentors through his life, the person who has most influenced him is his "big brother" Dale Kelly. They met 25 years ago through the Big Brothers Organization and are still best friends today.

He also calls Jesus the Ultimate Mentor, and says Jim Rohn is his favorite philosopher. Tracy credits his mother Freda with being a primary influence in his life; her ability to overcome major obstacles in her life provided inspiration for her son.

Tracy achieved a profit after only his first month in business, and today enjoys the freedom of time and choices. Tracy is a real-life hero and example for anyone who is thinking of being his own boss. He proves it is possible to achieve your dreams. ■

Tony Kent

Age: 56

Family: Jessica, 22; Jason, 21; Justin, 14, Tara, 12. Jason and Jessica are the two youngest Double Diamonds in the fifteen-year history of Cell Tech.

Highest Education: One semester of college (Yale).

Year started business: 1995.

Type of business: Network marketing.

Market: Anyone looking for hope, health and freedom.

Number of employees : 4

Best month (gross revenues): Very close to six figures.

Hours worked per week during start-up: Every waking hour during hyper growth. "Many of my downline said they could never do as much as I did, but when my income climbed so steadily many regretted later to have not put in the time."

Hours worked per week now: Tony says that depends on what you consider your business. He spends every waking hour developing himself, and all of this comes to manifestation in his business. He believes it is more about being, than doing, which is why we are called human beings and not human doings. He has been focusing the last year or two on writing a book and developing his seminar business. The next few months he is returning to focus directly on building again. He has decided to start building a second downline with a new company.

Favorite business magazines: *Upline, Success Magazine, Entrepreneur*

Favorite business books and authors: The Koran, Wallace B. Wattles, Deepak Chopra.

Relaxes by: Living life fully.

Keeps in shape physically by: He just put in a lap pool and plans to swim every day.

Favorite part of business: Helping people to help themselves.

Least favorite part of business: If there is ever something he doesn't like to do he hires someone to do it that is good at it.

Companies admired: Amway for forging the way.

Favorite quotes:

"Nothing so affects the life of a child as a parent's unfulfilled life." *(Jung).*

"The love you give is the love you get."
(Sidi Sheik Mohammed al-Jamal ar-Rifa'i).

"You can't build a business bigger than yourself." *(Tony Kent).*

Tony Kent checks out his interview in Six-Figure Income Magazine

Photographer Finds Magic in Network Marketing

BY JAN WALLEN

Tony Kent started out as a fashion photographer in Paris. He credits this experience with teaching him about the benefits of personal responsibility. Today he is using that knowledge to help others achieve personal growth and independence.

Along the way, he has earned many honors including Cell Tech Double Diamond, Relay 2000 Trainer, and Chairman of Cell Tech Solution Projects Team, a program which helps feed malnourished people throughout the world. He is also an author, has created audio and video tapes, and has created numerous tapes and other building tools for helping others become successful in network marketing. In addition, he has created *Magical Moments* which is a one man stage show using magic as a metaphor. The theme is about creating magic in our lives.

After beginning in network marketing, he continued to reinvest his checks, and began to turn a profit after about six months. He still invests heavily in lead programs for his downline. He runs ad co-ops and is diversifying more and more. Tony says, "I absolutely love mixing warm and cold markets."

Even though he has always been in business for himself, Tony says he likes network marketing because it leaves him free to create his own destiny.

Some of his publications include *Walking in Awareness*, a book about personal growth and transformation through network marketing; and *Paths of Power*, a video/audio program containing the material from his all-day seminars. He is also the author of a workbook on reaching your company's first serious level including recommended daily activities and necessary generic tools; a tape, *The History and Truths of Network Marketing*; as well as a booklet which summarizes his seminars, *Paths of Power*.

While his may sound like a magical, storybook story, Tony Kent is very real indeed. And he is committed to helping others succeed in his chosen industry. ∎

To purchase the books/tapes mentioned in this article,

...call 888-236-2515 or by fax at 505-983-2232 at my web site which is tonykent.com where you can read four chapters from my book and sample the audio and video tapes.

Trevor Levine

Age: 31

Family: None

Highest Education: 4 years college - Bachelor of Music

Year started business: 1993

Type of business: Helps business owners make more money with their marketing efforts; writing advertising copy, designing Websites, generating Website traffic, etc. If you happen to have an existing customer list, we can show you how to make a ton of money doing back-end offers.

Market: Businesses and entrepreneurs who want to generate more leads or make more sales using direct response advertising (i.e. print ads, direct mail, Internet marketing, etc.)

Number of employees: None, but subcontract a lot of work.

Best month (gross revenues): $21,378

Hours worked per week during start-up: "During our start-up phase - when I was focused on network marketing - I was working 25 hours per week for a telemarketing firm. That was my 'day job'. I had Wednesdays off, so I spent all day every Wednesday, Saturday, and Sunday building my business, not to mention most of the other 4 evenings."

Hours worked per week now: 35-40

Favorite business magazines: Marty Chenard's newsletter, *Advanced Direct*

Marketing. Tom Schreiter's newsletter, *Big Al's Recruiting Newsletter.* Jonathan Mizel's newsletter, *The Online Marketing Letter.*

Favorite business books and authors: Stephen Covey's *The 7 Habits of Highly Effective People* is the best book I've ever read.

Relaxes by: Taking hot baths and occasionally spending time in the woods - away from civilization. He also cooks occasionally (Hearty soups being his specialty.); "It's meditative for me,"

Keeps in shape by: Working out at a gym twice a week.

Favorite part of job: "Schmoozing with other really bright entrepreneurs – people who are on the cutting edge. And, writing killer ad copy."

Least favorite part of job: Dealing with the mundane administrative stuff.

Companies admired: "Among network marketing companies, I most admire Cell Tech. So many "health oriented" network marketing companies espouse health, but when you go to their conventions, they serve you with the kind of typical-American-diet food that causes arthritis, heart disease, stroke, and cancer. They're promoting a quick fix, not the genuine solution. Cell Tech is one of a very small handful of network marketing companies whose values are in alignment with its stated mission. One of the only companies that promotes a healthy, plant-based diet."

Favorite quotes:

"Without a dream, there's no reason to practice. Without practice, there's no reason to dream." *(I saw this on the back of a shirt.)*

Writer and Musician Turns Entrepreneur

BY JAN WALLEN

Trevor Levine wanted freedom - the freedom of not having to worry about an income; the freedom of time to pursue his passion for writing and for music. He found this freedom by creating a residual income through Network Marketing. And he is no slouch when it comes to his entrepreneurial efforts either.

He was featured in the 1997 "Who's Who of Professionals." In addition to his main entrepreneurial efforts, he is also an executive Consultant with an ancillary company that helps network marketers with qualified leads and ongoing training. He attended Randy Gage's first-ever MLM/Network Marketing Boot Camp.

Although it took him 16 months to begin making a profit, today he enjoys the benefits of a residual income. He has all the time he wants to write and to perform music. He lists other benefits such as not having to answer to anyone, no alarm clocks, and working when he wants to.

The person who most influenced the development of his values was his mother. "She also bought me a piano when I was 10. That was the start of my involvement with music."

Trevor says he has three heroes. The first is Stephen Covey. "Since reading The Seven Habits, I've looked to him as an extremely wise person. He possesses and is able to convey what it takes to lead a successful life."

Another influence for Trevor is Tom Schreiter. "Not only is Tom one of the savviest marketers I know, but he's also a very giving man who's always made himself available to offer me advice - even when I was, relatively speaking, a 'nobody.'"

His third hero is Jonathon Mizel. "Jonathon, too, has been a mentor to me. As I honed my ad writing skills, he'd critique my ads and sales letters, and fill me in on the 'inside secrets' of writing ad copy. There's one other thing I like about Jonathon. He really ENJOYS being an entrepreneur. Whenever I call him, he sounds like he is having a great time."

Trevor is also a person who enjoys what he does. He says that even with a residual income in place he continues to work 35 to 40 hours per week. Time, money and a passion - Trevor now has the freedom to pursue his interests as he wishes. He is an inspiration for entrepreneurs everywhere. ■

Jim McAfee

Age: 51

Family: Single.

Highest Education: B.A. in English Literature and a Th.M. in Semitics (4 years college, 4 years graduate school). Jim is also a Certified Clinical Nutritionist.

Year started business: Jim's mother, Lucille (pictured with Jim above) started the business in 1969. Jim joined her in 1974.

Type of business: Golden Neo-Life Diamite markets nutritional supplements, skin care, and cleaning compounds.

Market: "Everyone needs what we have to offer."

Number of employees: One full-time office manager and one part time in addition to mother, Lucille, and sister, Kharlyn.

Best month (gross revenues): $65,000.

Hours worked per week during start-up: about 30

Hours worked per week now: about 30

Favorite business magazines: *Upline, Fortune*

Favorite business books and authors: *Success Journey* by John Maxwell (favorite author), *Building the Leaders Around You* by John Maxwell, *The Five Love Languages* by Gary Chapman

Relaxes by: Travel, organic gardening, reading, contra dancing, guitar.

Keeps in shape physically by: Gardening, cycling, walking, contra dance

Favorite part of job: Creating ways to enable others to experience success and to develop success patterns.

Least favorite part of job: Accounting.

Companies admired: Microsoft; Hewlett Packard; Intel.

Favorite quotes:

"Loving people precedes leading them. People don't care how much you know until they know how much you care." (John Maxwell)

"Living itself is a risky business. If we spent half as much time learning how to take risks as we spend avoiding them, we wouldn't have nearly so much to fear in life." (E. Paul Torrance)

"You've got to get up every morning with determination if you're going to go to bed with satisfaction." (George Horace Lorimer)

Jim and Lucille McAfee were featured in the Sept/Oct '98 issue of Six-Figure Magazine

Amazing Turnaround

Jim McAfee was 27 years old when he discovered network marketing and has now been involved for 30 years. Prior to becoming involved with networking, he had companies tell him he was "overqualified" for jobs they were offering--eight years of college and graduate school did not seem to help a whole lot in getting a satisfying job. He found himself taking long commutes in rush hour traffic, working long hours, underpaid, and having to perform dangerous duties on some of his jobs. Jim realized that he was working to pay his own salary and also make a profit for his employers.

Jim was hesitant about becoming involved in network marketing in the beginning. He did not see himself as a "salesman." His mother, Lucille, encouraged him to give it a try. She showed him how to work from his strengths. Network marketing proved to be a wonderful opportunity. His teaching and communication skills made training distributors fun. He enjoyed working from his home and controlling his own future.

A special reward of network marketing is the ability to choose who one wishes to work with and who one desires for customers. Working with a nutrition company, one is associated with others who wish to improve their own health and better the lives of others.

Jim has been particularly impressed with the work of John Maxwell and others who emphasize the importance of leadership development. He feels it is a great experience to help others make strides in personal development and "grow" into success. The opportunity for continuous personal growth is an important part of the benefit of working for oneself.

Jim has received considerable recognition and rewards from the company he works with. These rewards include trips to London, Munich, Barcelona, Rome, Hawaii and numerous other locations. He has received many trophies and beautiful jewelry. The best part of working with an international company is making friends all over the world.

Being in business for oneself has been great for this overachiever. It has provided an opportunity to build a business which expands all over the world. ■

The Interviews

Brian Biro
(BB)

Marty Challenger
(MC)

Tracy Dieterich
(TD)

Tony Kent
(TK)

Trevor Levine
(TL)

Jim McAfee
(JM)

GETTING STARTED:

I'm starting a home business next month. I have a maximum of $3000 in start-up capital. Where should I invest it?

BB: The best possible thing to do with your $3,000 is to not spend it at all! Instead, take your business concept and get creative. Ask yourself, "Who will benefit the absolute most from my products or services?" When you are really clear about who your customers are – then ask yourself, "How can I approach these people with a true win-win opportunity wherein THEY basically finance my business start-up and I provide them with a service or product that improves their life or business. Spend $200 on some incredible books and read them many times: First, buy books by Chuck Whitlock. He is the absolute best when it comes to creative financing. Second, buy *Think and Grow Rich* by Napoleon Hill, *You Were Born Rich* by Bob Proctor, and *Beyond Success.* Your REAL start-up capital is your innovative idea, clear vision, and personal responsibility!

MC: Advertise! Advertise! Advertise! You may have the best widget in the world, with the best price, etc., etc., but... if your market does not know about you, how are they going to become your customers or future clients?

TD: Invest in education for yourself to advance the learning curve... books, tapes, rallies

TK: Speak with your best upline builder and ask their advice. I suggest always choosing things that feel good to you.

TL: A tried-and-true low-cost marketing plan works like this. You place low cost classified or lead generating ads. You can place this in magazines or on the Internet. (TIP: Only place your ad in places where several similar ads ALREADY appear; this means that others have already tested these media and found them to be profitable.) The typical lead generating ad offers a FREE REPORT and contains an 800 number. When people call, simply capture their name and address with a voicemail box. Then you mail them a killer sales letter which convinces them to buy what you're selling and send you money.

If you don't already have a compelling sales letter, call us for a quote. If you're not sure that your sales letter is as good as it can be, we can give you a critique. (Normally, we charge $250 for a critique, but if you let us know that you're a reader of SFI, we'll critique your letter for just $67.)

Here's a variation on the above method: In addition to, or instead of an 800 number, include a fax-on-demand number (and/or a Website address). Then your prospects can see your sales letter immediately. Doing this will save you the administrative time you would've had to spend taking requests off voice-mail, stuffing and mailing out envelopes, etc. Not to mention the costs of postage and printing. If you're interested in setting up a Website, call us for a quote.

JM: Need product for inventory, business cards, audiotapes for learning and to loan, checking account for the business.

I've just started a home business. My spouse has given me six months to make it work. Any advice?

BB: First of all, if your spouse is giving you six months to make your business work, I would start by really working and talking together with your spouse about the kind of commitment you want to make and the kind of support for each other you feel will create success. Unconditional support is an amazing, powerful source of inspiration.

MC: Your spouse is your partner in life and your partner at home. It only seems natural to share your excitement, enthusiasm and goals. I suggest having a six month goal and plan of action program written down with a deadline for its attainment. Be sure your goals are realistic and attainable. Then just do it!

TD: Have patience, it takes more than 6 months to develop a successful business of any kind. you have to think long-term – a college education takes 4 years before you even start working.

TK: I would ask for more understanding and support from your spouse. Share from your heart how important their support is to you and make them your most ardent supporter.

TL: Some businesses, by their nature, pay you a lot of money right away. For example, copywriting. You spend a week writing a sales letter, and get paid a few thousand dollars. Other businesses – like network marketing – pay off gradually, over time. This is why it took me 16 months to turn a profit; network marketing used to be my primary business. It was hard work, and it took patience, but it did pay off. So, if you choose network marketing – or something like it – be sure your spouse realizes that the pay off may not come within 6 months.

They say it takes money to make money. Should I try to get a small business loan for my start-up capital or just try to get by with my own limited finances?

BB: Having money to create more money is nice, but we're missing the best solution. Rather than a loan, once again consider the idea of creative financing where you identify who will win the most from your new business and you create a way for THEM to finance your venture – always being sure they will gain immensely in the process. I am not saying, look to them for LOANS. Instead I'm suggesting you find ways for those who will benefit the most from your business, and/or distribution channels who will win big from your business idea to pay for the services or products you'll deliver up front rather than using your own money.

MC: I do not recommend getting a small loan to start a business. Most small businesses that fail in the first 6 months to one year do so because of failure to properly budget the money they do have. If you don't have the start-up capital to start your small business – wait until you do have it. You are more likely to budget more carefully with monies you earned & saved, rather than from monies you received from a loan.

TD: Try to keep debt low...only borrow to leverage yourself if you have the ability to repay it. Invest your time, not money – find a good mentor.

TK: Unless your upline is able to show you a proven return on investment I would suggest caution. I would want to know more about a person before being able to suggest what to do. For one person I might say yes and for another I might say no. People have different levels of prosperity consciousness. I think that it is entirely possible to build a business without a loan.

TL: If you have an MBA and a formal business plan – in other words, if you really know what you're doing – then yes, get a loan or look for investors. If not – if you're doing this part time and you don't have a solid background in running a business – I would not recommend borrowing.

Do you consider yourself an "early adopter" of new technology?

BB: I am not an early adopter when it comes to technology.

MC: Yes, I do. The information program I developed makes everyone in my organization become an instant "heavy hitter"!

TD: Yes, I believe technology makes us more efficient and helps me to work smarter, not harder.

TK: Most definitely.

TL: Yes.

JM: We have been using many new technologies over the years. Others we have lagged on.

What is the primary use for your toll-free line?

BB: The primary use is as an order line for those purchasing my books, tapes, and other products.

MC: I use a toll-free number for my 24-hour recorded messages.

TD: Ad response, prospects to return calls, tape and product orders.

TK: For responses to advertising and sales of products.

TL: It's connected to a 2-minute voicemail message which details the network marketing support program I mentioned before – ProStep. If people like what

Technology Utilized

	Fax*	Toll-Free	Voice Mail	Computer	Email	Internet	Website
Brian Biro	✓	✓	✓	✓	✓	✓	✓
Marty Challenger	✓	✓		✓	✓	✓	
Tracy Dieterich	✓	✓	✓	✓	✓	✓	✓
Tony Kent	✓	✓	✓	✓	✓	✓	✓
Jim McAfee	✓	✓		✓	✓	✓	
Trevor Levine	✓	✓	✓	✓	✓	✓	✓

* Dedicated fax line

they hear, they call my office directly.

JM: Toll-free line is order line.

Describe your computer and peripherals used:

BB: I use a Power Macintosh G3 and a Global Village modem and Laserwriter printer.

TD: 486 Dell computer and HP laser printer.

TK: Main computer has 148 megs, 2 hard drives with 6.5 gig each, 20 inch monitor, IBM compatible, modem, fax, etc., plus 3 other computers. One an IBM laptop that I use for my multi-media seminar presentations. Two of the computers are networked. I also own two computers uniquely dedicated to tele-marketing. For peripherals, I have flatbed and slide scanners, a Ricoh digital camera, 2 color printers, 2 laser printers and one additional laser printer especially for postcard stock.

TL: Two Power Macintoshes networked via Ethernet. Operating System 7.6, plus a laser printer and 33.6 speed modems.

JM: 2 Pentiums and 2 486. A system for high resolution black and white output and faxing and scanning graphics. A system for color output and backup of office operating software. A system for internet communications and high resolution color output and databases of nutritional information. A system for running business software. For peripherals I have a scanner, a Jazz drive, Zip drives (2), and CD ROMS.

What software do you consider in the "must-have" category?

BB: Microsoft Word, NOW contact, Global Village Fax software, Quicken.

TD: Basics – nothing fancy is needed. Use KISS principle.

TK: Windows 95, Microsoft Word, Quickbooks, a good contact manager...I use Ascend, Act, My Mail Manager and a program designed strictly for my business that works with a genealogy that is sent through email. I also use Adobe Photoshop and Quark Xpress a lot.

TL: If you need to keep track of leads, prospects, customers, and/or distributors, you should definitely get contact management software. We use Filemaker Pro. Unlike ACT! and some of the others, Filemaker Pro is completely customizable. I also like Eudora for e-mail.

JM: Business software.

If you use the World Wide Web, name up to five personal favorite business URL's our readers can benefit from:

TD: www.mlm.com, www.money.com, www.tntmag.com, www.mmmonthly.com.

TK: I think this depends on each individual's taste. Use keywords to search within your interests.

TL: www.abdynamics.com, www.cyberwave.com, www.higherresponse.com, www.webletter.com.

Of all the technology you use, rank the top three:
BB: Phone, Fax, Computer
TD: Fax, 800 #, conference calling
TK: Phone, Computer, Fax
JM: Corel Draw and Corel Ventura as communication tools; Database searches for information; Computerized business operation

MARKETING & ADVERTISING:

Do you market on the Internet?
BB: My books are on Amazon.Com but other than that I only market on the internet by using it as an immediate mail tool to clients or potential clients who prefer internet as a means of communication. I do not cold market via internet. As a matter of fact, I don't really cold market!

MC: Not yet, but I certainly will as soon as I have it all set up. I will be up and rolling on the internet in early June.

TK: Yes, I use advertising to drive people to my site, as well as responsible, targeted e-mailing.

TL: Yes, currently, on www.webletter.com, my friend Declan Dunn offers his visitors a critique – from me – of their ads, sales letters, or web pages. Within the next couple of months, my own website should be up and running. The URL address will be www.marketingexperts.com

Do you use direct mail?
BB: My business is built via word of mouth. My only use of direct mail has been for special holiday offerings of my products or introduction of my new books.

MC: Yes I do. Direct mail works very good for my company! Because of the unique marketing methods I use, and because of the high income opportunity I represent, my direct marketing campaigns bring an average return of 22%-26% every time!

TK: Yes, extensively. I mail tapes, postcards, letters, etc. 50% or more of our revenues come from direct mail marketing.

TL: We mailed a recruiting letter to lists from Charles Possick and Tom Schreiter. That produced a 1.2% response and an 80% conversion rate. We also mailed a sales letter for my tape album, "Trade Secrets of The Ninja Network Marketer"; 1.8% of those who received that letter purchased the tapes. We are probably going to start mailing a postcard promoting ProStep to Possick's "heavy hitter" list.

Do you use print media?

BB: My only use of print media is as a writer or as someone the publication is writing a feature or interview article about.

MC: Yes, Card Decks.

TD: Newspapers and magazines, both locally and nationally.

TK: Yes. We do full-page ads, classifieds in newspapers and magazines, and I advertise meetings locally. Growth comes from a combination of a lot of different methods. My belief is that when you create action you never know how God will send it back. You might invest in a newspaper ad that draws no response but you meet a person at the market who turns into a great builder. Maybe you would not have met that person and drawn them into your business had you not made the effort of placing the ad.

TL: Yes. We run print ads for ProStep in the network marketing magazines. We've tested many types of ads – from classifieds to full-page ads. Currently, most of our ads are classifieds.

JM: Rarely use.

Approximately what % of your sales originate from print media marketing?

TD: 20%.

TK: It fluctuates.

TL: For ProStep, 100%.

JM: 5%.

Do you use radio and/or TV advertising?

BB: I do not use radio or TV advertising. However, I have appeared on over 300 radio talk shows and more than 30 television programs as a guest. This is wonderful promotion.

MC: I am going into radio advertising this summer!

TD: I have in the past, but you have to have someone who really knows that business because it is very expensive.

TK: I am doing some radio talk shows that promote my book and network marketing and want to do more.

TL: No.

JM: No.

What other kinds of marketing do you utilize?

BB: I have used book publicists to help secure media appearances.

MC: Fax Blasting and Email Blasting

TD: Seminars

TK: Warm market, trade shows, malls, parking lots, tape baskets, flyers.

TL: All of our clients (who've come to us for copywriting, website design, marketing help, etc.) have come from referrals. We make it easy for sphere-of-influence people (for example, people who write newsletters) to refer their subscribers or customers to us; we provide them with as many copies as they need of a one-page sales letter. This letter offers their subscribers or customers a critique – from me – of their ads, sales letters, or web pages. If a person who gets a critique decides to hire us, we send 15% of what they pay us to the referring party.

JM: Most of our business comes from lectures, loaning out tapes, one-on-one presentations, and word-of-mouth referrals.

Do you recommend using a toll-free number in advertising? Why or why not?

BB: I recommend a toll-free number particularly as an order line. I also believe deeply in extraordinary service. Potential clients and customers feel important when they are given a free number to call to learn about you.

MC: Yes I do. It's a known fact that more people will respond when there is a toll-free number than if not.

TD: Yes, you get more callers.

TK: Yes.

TL: Only in classified or small lead generating ads. And usually, to limit your liability, you should attach it to a short voicemail message. You can also limit your liability by being as specific as possible in your ad. In other words, instead of saying "Easy Money – Work From Home" (which will generate lots of UN-qualified responses), your ad might say "Free Network Marketing Report Reveals....". This way, only people with a SPECIFIC interest in network marketing will call you. You won't waste your money generating calls from people who have no interest in network marketing.

JM: We have not used because people tie up our order lines with long conversations. We would prefer to call them back.

Where do you market?

BB: My clients are primarily in the U.S. and Canada.

MC: I am now marketing locally & nationally.

TD: Locally, nationally and internationally.

TK: U.S., Canada, worldwide for my book and other products. I also have a number of distributors who retail product abroad so they have a base for building when there is international expansion.

TL: Nationally.

JM: All over the U.S. and in 50 world markets.

THE HOME OFFICE:

How should someone set up their home office to maximize its effectiveness?

BB: The home office should reflect YOUR spirit. It's important to keep an organized space and one that feels great to go to each day. I'm an unusual person to ask about this because I utilize a large space in my home that has my office on one half and my children's play room on the other. For me, that's a dream come true. I love having them nearby. If I need quiet for an interview or to concentrate the kids are quite comfortable with giving me that quiet time.

MC: Definitely have a separate room, preferably with a door to block out distracting noises and to assure privacy.

TD: Comfortable, simple and efficient – make your office a separate place in the home, but a place where you want to go.

TK: This is very personal...I surround myself with things I love...I have a wonderful salt water aquarium, a stand for my pet parrot, a bed for my dog, lots of books and photos...I like to be in an environment that feels good... my office is a reflection of who I am.

TL: The basics include a computer, a modem, a printer, file cabinets, a fax machine (with a DEDICATED fax line), a telephone headset, and either "call waiting" or "rollover voicemail." One thing I cannot stand is calling someone and getting a busy signal. That smacks of unprofessionalism. Same thing when I can't send a fax. So keep a dedicated fax line, a dedicated modem line, and a dedicated voice line. You must convey a professional image; these additional lines are worth the small extra cost. Here in California, the local phone company offers a "message center" service for $6.50 per month. It's a voicemail box connected to my main phone number, and when someone calls while I'm on the line, they get "rolled over" into the voicemail box. As a result, no one gets a busy signal. If your local phone company offers this feature, get it. I also recommend reading books on organization and time management. These will help you design your office ergonomically and for maximum efficiency.

JM: Keep the office part of the business as separate as possible from the living area. In a previous office we had our business downstairs and the living area upstairs. That worked well. You do not want customers walking through your living area to get products if you can help it.

Are there any ground rules you've established for yourself, family, etc. for operating at home successfully?

BB: The only rules are about the times when I require quiet and concentration. The other rule is that my office is pretty much off limits for ME at night because I choose to be with my family instead. If I'm excited about something

I'm working on I may go back into my office after everyone is asleep or very early in the morning. I believe that BALANCE is a must to live a truly abundant life and seek to have my office and work reflect that belief.

MC: No T.V. during work hours! My children have been taught to respect my work at home business, and they know that it is no different than if I worked outside the home. Your business is your business no matter where it is conducted.

TD: Schedule time off – everyone needs a break...it makes you more productive.

TK: No, I allow and encourage total freedom...my kids can feel now when it is permissible to interrupt.

TL: When I'm "at work," I turn off the ringer for my personal line. And when I'm "done with work," I turn off the ringer on the business line, and turn on the personal line. If possible, I recommend using a separate room for your home office. That way you can close the door when you want to "go home."

JM: We set regular office hours to discourage people from calling around the clock or coming by the home any time they want.

Do you consider working at home an advantage or disadvantage to your business overall?

BB: Working at home is an enormous advantage to my business – and an even BIGGER advantage to my LIFE!

MC: Working at home is definitely an advantage! Unless I am conducting business out of town, I have no commute, no bridge fares, no commute congestion, no all day garage fees, & I'm never late to work! Oh yeah, I really can work in my pajamas if I want!

TD: It is a great advantage...no commute, no dress code, and it is much more efficient than a traditional office.

TK: Total advantage.

TL: There are pros and cons. It does save money. However, if you find yourself working all the time, it may be worth having your office in a separate physical space. For some people, that's the only way they can truly "get away from it."

JM: Working at home is a great advantage. It shows people they can be at home with their family and earn an income.

MANAGEMENT STYLE:

Do you farm out any of your work?

BB: I farm out a lot of my work. However, never farm out the work that you truly enjoy and that is at the heart of your purpose. I seek to farm out the areas I'm not very good at and don't have passion. I want to create time and value leverage by finding people who LOVE to do the things I don't and giving them the ball!

MC: No, and I recommend that you never farm out telephone return calls when the person being called back definitely expects to hear from me, rather than an assistant.

TD: No.

TK: Yes, a lot; productions of all audio and video tapes, almost all color printing in quantity, some graphics work, web page design, manual printing, packaging, etc.

TL: I farm out bookkeeping and a lot of administrative work. When we did big mailings, I hired people to stuff and stamp the envelopes. If you can afford to hire other people, I recommend adopting this attitude: "Anything that doesn't have to be done by me shouldn't be done by me."

JM: Yes, our audio and video production and often printing is done by others.

Do you encourage or discourage partnerships?

BB: I much prefer strategic alliances to partnerships in business. Partnerships CAN work but it is critical to set the ground rules up completely clearly and to REALLY communicate. It demands a "we go" versus an "ego" mentality. In a strategic alliance I just feel a higher level of freedom.

MC: I do not encourage partnerships. There is a whole gamut of problems that can and do arise from a partnership business, especially if the business is home based.

TD: I discourage partnerships – they are very difficult to make work long-term... like a marriage. I had one business partnership and it was good and bad – it only lasted 9 months. Form strategic alliances with people who can help you, and build good friendships.

TK: Encourage mostly.

TL: I can't advise others on this. I personally have not entered any partnerships.

JM: Discourage partnerships – we have seen too many nasty fights.

Do you encourage or discourage hiring family members?

BB: Hiring family members is great for a business like mine – IF they want to participate. As a business grows, I think it is critical that family members are not given special treatment (though EVERYONE should feel they are treated as someone special!). Have family members earn respect of other team members through their performance, spirit, and energy.

MC: I do encourage hiring family members. Although, I think this decision should be carefully scrutinized. A lot depends on what kind of business you have and the responsibilities that go with it. Family members should definitely be this area.

TD: Family members can offer trust, but be careful... most of the time family members are not good employees.

TK: I love working with my kids...when I grew up I hardly ever had a chance to see my dad work...I am really proud that both my older kids reached the top level of Cell Tech, the youngest in the 14-year history of the company... working with them has been one of the most rewarding things in my life...my younger kids love to work with me doing mailings or whatever they can do... Cell Tech is like one big embracing family... I travel a lot with my kids... bring them to our company celebrations, to my seminars, to company functions... they are always embraced with open arms... it's really wonderful to have not seen this anywhere else in the industry. I like the feel of the new company that I just got started with as well.

JM: Hiring family members – works great if the family members are interested in the business and capable.

When legal issues arise, what's your usual response?

BB: Fortunately I haven't had any real problems to deal with in this area. Over the years, however, my belief is that the best way to deal with legal problems is to treat people so well and so honestly up front that the issues will not come up. If they still do, be honest, clear, and above all, keep your perspective and purpose always in mind.

MC: Be calm. Analyze the issue and see how it will benefit your situation. Then proceed to make that benefit the issue.

TD: Try to work out any legal issues before an attorney gets involved.

TK: I have not had any at all so far...If I did I would immediately contact my company and if necessary hire an extremely competent lawyer...I do not want or envision any legal challenges and there should not ever be a challenge if one acts ethically, honestly, and with high moral standards.

TL: I call my attorney for advice on how to handle the situation. More often than not, he doesn't get involved. He just advises me.

MONEY & INVESTMENTS:

Does earning a lot of money improve the quality of your life, and if so, in what ways?

BB: Earning a greater income does allow our family to enjoy more freedom when it comes to travel, to living where we choose, and to giving. We have pretty simple wants, though and always remember that happiness is not determined by your finances. More important to me is being able to earn the income we desire without spending all my waking hours working. Money is a tool, but happiness is a choice! I believe in abundance and that the greatest benefit of earning a higher income is being able to give more generously to those I love, and to causes we believe in.

MC: Yes it does! Sophie Tucker once said:... "I've been rich, and I've been poor, and let me tell you something – rich is much better"!

TD: YES... money can be a good thing – it gives you security, peace of mind, financial freedom, and allows you to live totally debt free and really help others. There are many good causes that need more money. But, be careful, money only makes you more of what you already are.

TK: Money is a wonderful tool for spiritual growth...learning how to expand inwardly to accept abundance into our lives creates new worlds to explore and with this spiritual growth comes an improved quality of life. I like to surround myself with beauty, I like to spend my time focusing on things other than financial worries and I love to be able to help others and facilitate their growth.

TL: Yes. It gives me more freedom than I'd otherwise have. It allows me to hire other people to handle my administrative work; that frees me up to produce more revenue. It allows me to record my songs in a professional recording studio, rather than trying to record them at home, etc.

JM: Money is a tool which makes it possible to accomplish what one wishes to accomplish. It provides the ability to help others in many ways.

Best general tax advice?

BB: The most important tax advice I could offer is simply to be meticulous and organized about your records, and to find high integrity, high quality tax advisors.

MC: Hire the best tax consultant you can. One who will keep you informed on tax codes, changes, best investments for your home business, and most of all:... a consultant who has your concerns as priority in legally reducing your taxes to the lowest amount allowed by law.

TD: Use a professional, but stay involved yourself. All of us need to have some general knowledge of tax issues.

TK: Get a good accountant.

TL: When you pay someone else to do work that you could've done, you don't have to pay taxes on that money. Whereas if you were to do that work yourself, you WOULD have to pay taxes on it. So, in effect, if you pay someone $9/hour, it only costs you about $6/hour. You would've paid 30-40% of that money in taxes.When you go out to eat with a large group of people, discuss business with them. Then you can pay for the meal on your credit card and write it off as a business expense.

JM: Obtain a copy of business writeoffs from the IRS. Businesses have expenses which is a tax advantage not available to someone working at a job.

Best general investment advice?

BB: When it comes to investment my simple advice is to heed the advice of *Think and Grow Rich* – pay yourself, and feed your investments first and always spend less than you earn. If you stay with it and find a balance of risk and security that feels good to you, you will win in the long run.

MC: My best general investment advice is to always invest in yourself. If you have reached financial independence and are now comfortable with your monthly income, get in the habit of putting 25% away for your retirement. Better yet – try to put yourself in that habit now!

TD: Keep your eyes open and get as much knowledge as you can... read and learn from others who make a lot of money. Some professionals try to teach you how to invest, but they have little results themselves.

TK: Invest in things that you believe in and want to support... then if you don't make money you can feel good that you invested in something of value.

TL: Owning your own home is a great tax shelter.

JM: Invest in solid things with a long track record. Don't try to get rich quick – you are more likely to lose money.

You're in business already, and you've just received a windfall of $20,000. What would you do with it?

BB: Give at least $5,000 to charity, or important people in my life who are in need. Some will think this brainless, but I am absolutely certain that every time I give unconditionally and without any concern about what I might receive back, greater abundance flows into my life. The rest of the "windfall" would be used for family needs, investment, and product development.

MC: $5,000 would go into my retirement fund, $5,000 would go into my teenage children's retirement fund! (How many teenagers do you know that have retirement funds set up for them?) $2,000 (10%) would go to church tithes, $6,000 would be put back into the business for additional successful advertising, and $2,000 would go into our weekend get away or vacation account.

TD: I would tithe 10% and invest the rest in Vanguard mutual funds.

TK: This would depend on my cash flow situation...I would do something with it that would multiply it.

TL: Take some time out to finish designing our website. Buy faster computers. I'd also invest some of it in things, or systems, that would save us time and enable us to be more productive.

JM: Use the money to build a customer base or acquire inventory.

What do you lead with–your company's products or the business opportunity?

TD: Opportunity

TK: Whichever is most appropriate...I never encourage anyone to do networking with a company if they don't feel great about the products.

JM: We usually lead with the company products unless it is clear the individual is looking for a business opportunity.

Rank the following traits in order of their importance in building a successful network marketing business: enthusiasm, persistence, knowledge, communication skills.

TD: Persistence, Enthusiasm, Communication Skills, Knowledge

TK: Enthusiasm, persistence, communication skills, knowledge...I put knowledge last because people don't care how much you know until they know how much you care.

JM: Enthusiasm, Communication skills, Persistence, Knowledge

How long were you in network marketing before you saw your first four-figure commission check? Five-figure check?

TD: 6 months, 1 year

TK: I dabbled around for a few years with other companies... did see a four-figure check in one of them after a month or two. When I found Cell Tech it all clicked... it was like coming home... my thoughts, feelings, ideas were all in alignment with the vision of the company and the people involved... everything clicked and my first month's check was well over what I had ever made elsewhere. My first five figure check was just a few months later. I am experiencing the same feeling with the new downline I'm building. I love the product and it really helps people and everything is flowing. I reached a four-figure check in my second week. There are always challenges, but they are part of our growth process. I was always taught that you should only build one business at a time, but I am sensing a paradigm shift in our industry about this. I don't believe that I could start two downlines at once effectively, but now that I have an established downline I feel able to start a second one. Besides I believe that I can share a lot of product with both downlines because they are both connected in many ways. The products that I like to share are natural and effective and there is a similarity in the type of people I attract. One company has what I believe to be far and away the most powerful food that one can put in their body to build a strong immune system and experience the benefits of greater energy and clarity of mind, while the other company has 100 percent natural, homeopathic patches that work with weight loss and weight control, as well as patches for stress and sleep that are about to be released.

JM: Four Figure: 2 months; Five figure: 6 months.

What's more important –the initial contact with a prospect or the follow-up?
TD: Follow-up

TK: The founder of Cell Tech, Daryl Kollman once told me that there is no greater organism... everything has it's divine purpose... initial contact and follow up are the same... they are both important.

JM: Most important – Follow up determines what will eventually happen with the prospect.

You've just recruited a promising new distributor – how do you help them get off to a good start –or do you consider that the new distributor's responsibility?
TD: It's my responsibility, but I only work with people who deserve it... not need it. You cannot push a rope!

TK: I work with them to help them get clear on why they are doing the business and what is their purpose... once I know this I help them create goals that are in alignment with their purpose.

JM: We work with the new distributor to find what way of building a business would work best for them with their talents and background. Everyone is different.

How do you get your best leads?
TD: Advertising in local newspapers – you find people who are looking for an opportunity and ready to get started.

TK: I create them through intention... everything I do, I do from the insider first... I explore many different strategies to get leads but clearly knowing what I want is what creates the best leads.

JM: One-on-one conversations.

I'm planning a big local meeting. What's the best way to fill the room?

TD: Promote, promote, promote! Find leaders who are willing to have enough one-on-one meetings and home meetings to get prospects to the hotel meeting as a follow-up step.

TK: Word of mouth, advertising, phone calls and targeted emailing.

JM: Have several well-known and popular speakers. Get lots of people involved in putting the meeting on.

I need to generate a hundred leads within 60 days. What's my best strategy to achieve this?

TD: Newspapers can be expensive, but they are the best way to get leads fast.

TK: Choose a system that pleases you...If people hate cold calls they won't be very good at it... if they are scared to invest in advertising, that won't work well... again, intention is a strong tool... decide what kinds of leads you want and create the space internally for these leads. There are so many ways to get leads that I believe any system works better when you love it. If someone puts a tape basket in a gym, and loves going to the gym, their basket will reflect this energy... someone might put fresh flowers everyday with a wonderful photo of themselves, smiling, with their kids and full of tapes with a wonderful label and offer a free prize from a drawing later of everyone who leaves their name and phone, while someone who doesn't really like the gym and hardly ever goes there is going to create a basket with a less inviting energy which will generate fewer leads. I always believe that quality is better than quantity. I ask during my seminar if people would rather have someone like me who can build a downline or 100 consumers... no one yet has chosen the 100 consumers.

JM: Ask for referrals.

How many distributors must a person recruit each month to succeed in network marketing?

TD: Everyone has a different philosophy on how many people you must recruit personally to be successful. My theory is that you need to find 1-2 per month to really find a few leaders that will stay with you long-term, and who have desire to do what it takes. The quality of prospects has changed over the years... in the olden days, you could sponsor 10-12 people total and make a fortune – not anymore!

TK: Again, it's not quantity but quality... to succeed in network marketing one should never stop sponsoring... when sponsoring stops at the top, it stops underneath... I just experienced this in my own organization... I stopped sponsoring for a while and lost a lot of people... that is why I am committed to going back and sponsoring again... depending on the marketing plan, 2-3 strong legs can create a 6-figure income so I suggest to keep sponsoring until you have these legs... I also have put a lot of people under my good builders... it's my way of showing them I care.

JM: Those who recruit 3 a month seem to become successful on a regular basis.

Best tips for surviving rejection?

TD: Read books, listen to tapes, go to all the meetings and functions. Also, stay focused on your dreams!

TK: Rejection is not often personal. People are saying no to a product or opportunity, not so much to you as a person, and usually the no is because they don't really understand.

JM: Calculate how many people you need to talk to in order to get a yes. Consider each conversation a step toward that goal.

Do you recommend that new distributors prospect close friends and family?

TD: I recommend new distributors contact everyone, including family and friends because everybody knows someone else – that is the definition of net-working. However, you need to prepare your new distributor for rejection and help them with your knowledge and credibility.

TK: I recommend new people do what feels really good to them. If they want to go to their friends and warm market, I encourage it, and I arm them with lots of information about what happens when we encounter dream stealers... My mom has been my first recruit in a lot of my early ventures... she was always supportive and great.

JM: New distributors may not be very effective with close friends (it depends).

In five years I'll be....

BB: In five years I'll be loving every precious moment with my wife and children. Writing new books, creating new seminars, and touching as many lives as I can through my work while remembering to live with balance!

MC: In 5 years I'll be a multi-millionaire averaging 100 sales per month which translates into $100,000 per month!

TD: Traveling the world, building my business and speaking while I still have the desire. I've retired twice already, and I'm not ready to slow down yet...

TK: Five years from now I will be enjoying extremely good health, lots of energy, total financial freedom and will feel very good about having helped introduce thousands of people to the opportunity of hope, health and freedom. My four children are living the life of their dreams as well.

TL: Working 25-30 hours per week. Working with a few big clients on a percentage-of-sales basis.

JM: In five years I'll be doing the same thing I am now and loving it. We will have built our educational division to much greater size than it is now.

In ten years I'll be...

BB: In ten years I'll be doing even more of the same! I love what I do and am thrilled with the idea of continuing to grow in these areas I've chosen to focus on.

MC: In 10 years I'll be semi-retired, traveling the world regularly, and living the good life. I'll be on the lecture circuit throughout the United States teaching others how to "duplicate" the exact same successful things I do – so they may experience the exact same success.

TD: Semi-retired with a family, managing my investments and doing charity work. Maybe I'll write a book?

TK: In ten years all my children will be totally independent and have learned and mastered many of the principles of manifestation that I have been sharing with others. I continue to be connected to source energy, having mastered the same principles myself. I have helped to bring my guide's teaching to thousands of people, and spend most of my time working with causes and ideas that touch my heart. I tithe on a regular basis, giving abundantly. My income is managed in a responsible and fruitful manner. I have learned and continue to learn and share unconditional love. Network Marketing has grown and continues to grow as a viable and honest industry, whose people practice, encourage and teach responsible global stewardship. Network marketing is a force that has helped to redistribute wealth to people who use their abundant financial resources to create a better world. I am making a difference.

TL: Financially independent and semi-retired. Spending most of my time writing music and exploring other personal interests.

JM: In ten years I'll be doing the same thing I am now on much more of a worldwide scale. We would like to have a presence in all the markets available to us.

What most motivates you in building your business?

BB: Serving people, touching lives, and feeling I am living what I have been put on earth to do.

MC: The ability to earn $1,000 – $2,000 everyday right from the comfort of my home, and the ability to successfully communicate that ability to others.

TD: Recognition, other people's success.

TK: Helping myself and others to be the best that we can be and sharing the knowledge that connection with God is the most potent force that exists.

TL: Discovering bigger opportunities.

JM: The desire to help people become healthy and successful.

How often do you read books and/or listen to or watch tapes for improving your business skills or knowledge?

BB: I read quite a lot and listen to tapes occasionally.

MC: I get up every morning at 4:30. The first hour of every day for me is spent listening to Anthony Robbins, Brian Tracy, Les Brown & others whose educational materials inspire me to be the best I can be.

TD: Everyday, without fail – I read over 100 books each year.

TK: Everyday, all the time.

TL: Monthly

JM: Read books and listen to tapes daily.

The most underrated activity in business is?

BB: Giving!

MC: The most underrated activity in business has to be personal development. If I were to miss just one morning of not starting my day by listening to my mentors, I feel I would have done myself an extreme disservice.

TD: Prospecting

TK: It is not as much about doing as it is about being. An activity does not necessarily bring about desired results if it is not done in harmony with a higher purpose. Activity produces more positive results when it is performed with love and with passion. When love and passion are present, any activity is capable of being like a prayer and producing great results.

TL: Watering your plants

JM: Listening to what people have to say.

The most overrated activity in business is?

BB: Taking!

MC: Cold calling! A down-to-earth, right-to-the-point, tell-it-like-it-is, hard-hitting, honest, direct mail, fax blast or email piece of communication will always outperform the results of "cold calling"!

TD: Retailing

TK: Doing things without love, passion and faith.

TL: Managing other people

JM: Presenting the money opportunity. Many people are looking for more than money.

If you had to start your business all over again, what would you do differently?

BB: I would have started with more focus on my speaking. It has grown immensely since I decided to put more of my concentration towards my seminars and workshops.

MC: Nothing. The business is set up to be successfully "duplicated" by almost anyone. If you don't try to re-invent the wheel, your success in this business actually becomes "unavoidable"!

TD: Learn faster – find a mentor

TK: I would have hired more people early on to help with connecting my new people to our products. Retention is a major key to creating real walk away residual income in network marketing.

TL: I would have outsourced the fulfillment of my tape album. Selling that tape album was one of our first big projects, and it was very consuming. There was so much more administrative work than I had anticipated. Taking orders off voicemail, entering the orders into our database, processing credit cards, making trips to the print shop and post office, stuffing and sealing packages, dealing with bad checks and maxed out credit cards, etc. – it was a hassle!

JM: We would devote more time to training leaders.

What was your worst business decision?

BB: I selected one promoter that turned out to be a major mistake.

MC: Purchasing out dated so-called "Hot Lists"!

TD: Putting all of my eggs in one basket.

TK: I have learned something from every decision. So for me there is no such thing as failure or a "worst decision."

TL: Hiring Magnetix to fulfill orders. Yes, we came to a point where we did outsource the fulfillment – to a company called Magnetix – in Florida – the same company that was duplicating the tapes. I wasn't there to oversee what they did or didn't do, but we got lots of complaints from customers who had not received their tapes. Eventually, we moved the fulfillment back in-house!

JM: Forming a partnership with the wrong people.

What was your best business decision?

BB: Choosing to write my first book and to work at home!

MC: Making major changes in advertising techniques that now bring in a 20% positive return.

TD: Starting a library, starting to invest my money early.

TK: Constantly following my passions, doing what I love to do, being present, playing full out and constantly paying attention to living in harmony with Divine wisdom.

TL: Honing my ad writing skills. Once you know how to ultra-motivate people with the printed word, you can sell virtually anything.

JM: Choosing a company which was stable, was in the right industry, and had a long track record.

What do you consider to be the main keys of your success?

BB: I love people and believe that the greatest value I have to offer is through my principle-based training filled with fun, energy, and heart. I am a "world-class buddy thanker" and truly recognize and appreciate others. Most of all I have learned to look inside my own heart to know if I am successful. **Success to me is the peace of mind that comes from knowing I've given the best of which I'm capable.**

MC: I consider the main key to my success finding what works best, and then "duplicating" that same successful method, month after month.

TD: Faith, belief, persistence, enthusiasm, posture, drive, focus

TK: My love of God.

TL: Randy Gage's bootcamp was a turning point for me – that's where I learned the basics to writing ad copy and making money with direct response marketing. I also learned a lot from Tom Schreiter, Tom Mudry, and Jay Abraham. Ultimately, it was my friendship with Jonathan Mizel that put me on the road to making copywriting, marketing consulting, and Website design my primary business.

JM: We have great communication skills in both the nutrition field and also business presentation, a very professional operation, and a good reputation with customers and with the community.

What's your success philosophy?

BB: See the bolded part of previous answer.

MC: Establish your goals both in your mind and on paper. Set a deadline to meet your goals. (Write it on your calendar). Then, with no excuses of any kind accomplish that goal!!

TD: Put God first, work very hard and stay focused on one thing at a time.

TK: Know your purpose, why you are here on earth, and learn how to express it in less than a dozen words so that a ten-year-old can understand it. A lot of what I teach is based on this. I have worked out a system which is a kind of synthesis from many others that helps people be able to do this in a couple of hours. Then choose goals that are in alignment with that purpose and do what you choose to do with love in your heart.

TL: Learn what WORKS – never assume that the "marketing methods" taught by the company that put you in business will get you anywhere. (Usually, they won't.) Never assume that the ads or marketing materials they give you will work. If they really worked, why would the company need you? They could invest their OWN money running these ads. They could invest their OWN money implementing these methods. That's what a company with truly effective marketing materials would do. When, instead, they sell a "business opportunity" to you, YOU'RE the one who has to gamble your hard-earned dollars. In short, what you need MOST is a method of making sales that's ALREADY PROVEN TO WORK. If you don't already have compelling ads and marketing materials, call us for a quote. If you're not sure that your materials are as good as they can be, call us for a critique.

JM: If you help others get what they want, you will get what you want from life.

What about you has changed the most since finding success in business?
BB: I have become more balanced and less of a workaholic. I am living my word and my personal vision much more authentically.

MC: I have changed stress into energy & enthusiasm.

TD: I now have bigger dreams, stretch myself and am committed to helping people more than ever before. Also, I have a lot more investment knowledge and am grateful for all the blessings in my life.

TK: I am blessed in that I have always felt successful in business. When you enjoy the process, you are not attached to the outcome. If you enjoy the present, you will create a future that feels good. My passion is feeling connected to God, and staying connected. I want people to know that with God everything is possible. I have seen material wealthy people with virtually no real power, unable to connect to source energy. And every person of true spiritual power is capable of manifesting material well being if they so choose.

TL: I no longer worry about my future.

JM: The personal growth and growth in self-confidence has been tremendous.

What is the legacy you hope to leave?
BB: I want to be remembered first as a loving husband and father. Next, I hope to be remembered as a person who cared deeply about others, who came straight from his heart, and who helped people recognize that there is something remarkable in each of us.

MC: The legacy that I hope to leave is that Marty Challenger, (the man who coined the expression... "Tell-It-Like-It-Is") did just that. That he was totally committed in bringing out the best in others, and "proved" that commitment by "practicing what he preached" every day of his life.

TD: Security for my family that I never had and I hope to leave this world better than I found it by developing champions one person at a time.

TK: That I lived fully and inspired others to dream big and live a fulfilled life using spiritual principles to open our hearts and love unconditionally.

TL: That I helped hard-working business owners and entrepreneurs make all the money they possibly could.

JM: We want to leave a business to the third generation in our business and change the health and wealth of tens of thousands of people.

Chuck Branham

Age: 68

Family: Wife, Claudia. They have 10 children between them.

Highest Education: 3 years of college.

Employees: Five.

Year started business: 1993.

Type of Business: Network Marketing. He is an Independent Distributor for Nikken, Inc. (Magnetic and far infrared technology health products).

Best month (gross revenue): $76,131.79

Hours worked per week during start-up: About 20.

Hours worked per week now: About 20.

Favorite Business Magazines: *The Christian Businessman, Upline, Six-Figure Income*

Favorite Business Books/Authors: *The Bible, The Seven Habits of Highly Effective People* by Stephen Covey, *The Leadership Principles of Jesus* by Joe Batten and Gail Batten, *Becoming A Person of Influence* by John Maxwell and Jim Dornan

Relaxes by: Take short naps, reads, prays & meditates.

Favorite part of his business: Making positive differences in people's lives through his products and business opportunity.

Least favorite part of his business: Watching people give up their dreams.

Stays in shape by: Using a treadmill, various exercises, walking.

Admired Companies: Nikken, Inc., World Vision, Injoy

*One of Chuck Branham's homes
— a bonus he earned from Nikken.*

LOVE, HUGS AND SMILES

BY JAN WALLEN

Chuck Branham enjoys the love, hugs and smiles that come along with the freedom to earn a large income while helping others. He also enjoys having the freedom to travel and time to enjoy his family and friends. Network Marketing has made these things possible for Chuck, along with personal recognition and the giving and receiving of money.

As a Nikken distributor, Chuck has earned a great deal of recognition along the way. In 1994, he was number one in personal group volume for North America; he has been named a diamond Distributor, a member of the President's Club, and also received the company's Paragon Award. In addition to the recognition, he has earned an auto bonus and a home bonus.

Chuck's heroes are those closest to him – his parents and his wife. He cites their strength, character, and unconditional love as attributes that make them heroes. He also said his mother is the person who has most influenced his life.

This hard worker earned a profit his first month in the business. "I've wanted to be my own boss for many years," Chuck said. "I believe my Nikken business is an answer to my prayers."

Chuck is not only on the receiving end financially, but he also has established a separate business, Success Express, which exists to raise money for several charities. Success Express Inc caters to business people with books, tapes, and videos in the areas of sales, marketing, leadership, personal development, and motivation. Their specialty is materials for Network Marketers.

"We fund this business, and one of the main purposes is to raise money for charities that help children such as orphans. We don't intend to take any profit from this business," said Chuck, "but our intention is to give every penny to World Vision, Feed the Children, and several orphanages, including one in Nepal and one in Africa."

Success Express has one of the largest selections of books, tapes, and videos in its field in the world. They may be reached at 1-800-966-8887.

Chuck Branham is a person who exemplifies the traits of his heroes: strength, character, and unconditional love. ■

Robert Butwin

Age: 46

Family: Son Marc, 10; daughter Randi, 8; Wife Bonnie.

Highest Education: College Graduate

Year started business: 1984

Type of business: He started in network marketing in 1984. All his work in this industry has been with health & nutrition products.

Market: Anyone who wants to gain better health or improve their lifestyle because of the freedom that network marketing offers.

Number of employees : 1

Best month (gross revenues): $80,000 in personal income. Approximately 1.5 million dollars in sales.

Hours worked per week during start-up: About 40.

Hours worked per week now: About 25.

Favorite business magazines: *Upline, Money Makers Monthly, Network Trainer.*

Favorite business books and authors: Anything by Jim Rohn, tapes like *"Take Charge of Your Life."* He's a great speaker and has excellent points which are easy to relate to.

Relaxes by: Playing basketball five days a week. He also has his own meditation practice.

Keeps in shape physically by: Playing basketball, Cycling with his wife five days a week.

Favorite part of business: Watching the people he is mentoring create breakthroughs in their businesses. "Like what Maslow talked about regarding self-actualization. It's neat to see people you're mentoring become self-sufficient."

Least favorite part of business: When someone you are working with loses sight of their dream and gives up.

Companies admired: Royal Body Care Rainforest Bio-Energetics, Oxyfresh, Viva America. Robert feels they have good life changing products. "They each have a vision of where they are going, and they have heart-centered leadership. They all listen to the field, too, and that's very important."

Favorite quotes:

"You make a living by what you get. You make a life by what you give." (Winston Churchill)

"You don't have to be great to get started but you have to get started to be great." (Les Brown)

NO LIMITS

BY JAN WALLEN

Robert Butwin's goal in life is to be a no-limit person. After hearing Wayne Dyer's tape, *No Limit Person*, Robert realized that he had been creating limits in his life. "I've tried to become a no limit person. It started me on the path of what I've become today."

Robert went into business for himself after realizing that Corporate America would not allow him to live the kind of live he wanted. "There are so many limitations. They expected you to work so many hours per week and handle a lot of politics which I didn't like, so I started searching for an alternative way to have the freedom I wanted, a career that would enable me to experience life the way I wanted to live.

He is well on the way to realizing his goal, having been named Distributor of the Year from MLMIA for two straight years. He says that one of his heroes is John Glenn who inspired him by going into space at his age. Another no limit person.

Robert's path in Network Marketing has not always been easy. When he first started in this business, he went all out but lacked the proper mentorship to become successful. The net result was a lot of debt, six figures in fact. But Robert did not set limits on himself or give up on his dream. "I never gave up on the vision of the kind of lifestyle I could live through this business. ... Four years later, after finding the right kind of mentorship, I was able to clear up all my debts and walk away from my job and devote full time to my career in network marketing."

Having the right support system in place is crucial to success in any business. As shown in the career of Robert Butwin, it made all the difference in his level of success.

He says that the best thing about being self-employed is that he gets to make his own decisions. "The people I meet and work with are a joy and the differences I'm able to make in their lives is the greatest pleasure imaginable. I am able to make a difference in a lot of people's lives."

Robert has written a book called Street Smart Networking. He has also released two tapes: Getting Started in your Networking Business and The Secrets of the Money Funnel and How it Can Make You Rich. All are available through his office, and the book may also be purchased at bookstores. ∎

Dale Calvert

Age: 38

Family: Married for sixteen years to Stephanie. Three daughters, Brittanie, 15; Channing, 13; and Allie, 7.

Highest Education: He attended night classes at a local business college while working at IBM, until he got involved in network marketing. He believes that formal education will make you a living, self-education will make you a fortune.

Year started business: 1980; Full-time for the last 15 years.

Type of business: New Image International specializes in diet and weight loss products.

Market: He believes that in network marketing the real product is the people, the distributors. The market for weight loss products is obviously huge, 33+ BILLION $$! However, the real market is the frustrated men & women who are tired of trading time for dollars.

Number of employees: 4

Best month (gross revenues): You wouldn't believe me if I told you! The network marketing industry and the New Image International opportunity has made me a millionaire.

Hours worked per week during start-up: 80

Hours worked per week now: 60+, because he chooses to.

Favorite business magazines: *Upline, Working At Home, Success, Six-Figure Income.*

Favorite business books and authors: He enjoys all of John Maxwell's books such as *"Developing the Leaders Around You," "Raising a Giant"* by Bob Crisp; & *The Bible.*

Relaxes by: Traveling with his family & friends, especially to the Caribbean, Cancun & Hawaii.

Keeps in shape by: He takes massive supplements, treadmill, basketball.

Favorite part of business: He feels that network marketing gives the chance to live a life of significance because of the impact you can make on another person's life. His motivation is the opportunity to see his people walk across the stage, having reached the top position in the company.

Least favorite part of business: Dealing with ignorant self-centered people who think the world owes them something.

Companies admired: Amway, Shaklee & Mary Kay, each having been doing business for over 25 years.

Favorite quotes:

"Without continuous personal development you are now all that you will ever become, and hell starts when the person you are, meets the person you could have." (Eli Cohen)

"Success in this industry is not in finding the right person, but in becoming the right person." (Dr. Forrest Shaklee)

"He who wishes to be great, let him be the servant of many." (The Bible)

Audios & Videos By Dale Calvert:
VIDEOS:
   Confessions of a Network Marketing Millionaire – 3 Hour Video Training Program
   The Power of a Dream – 1 1/2 hour Video Training
   Finding the last Network Marketing Co. you will ever join – 2 Hr. Video Training
AUDIO CASSETTES:
   "The Secret to Network Marketing Success"
   "Why you Can't build a Network Marketing Company Mailing Cassette Tapes"
   "Network Marketing is a SCAM"

Rebel Finds Good Life In The Leadership Development Business

BY JAN WALLEN

Dale Calvert is a self-described rebel. "I didn't buy into 'going to school, get a good education and get a good job for a good company routine' just because everyone said that is what you are supposed to do."

He goes on to say, "I felt like most of the people I knew who had followed that advice were miserable, living their life for the weekends. I looked at the people that were working for someone else, and none of them had what I wanted! Owning my own business was the only option I had."

And for Dale Calvert, it has been a good option. He has received many awards including the One Percent club, Altuz Bird winner, Rookie of the Year, and President's advisory Council. "All individual awards are only possible because of a great team that pushes you to the top."

He started with Shaklee Corporation in 1984, and for three years, put every dime he made back into the business. At the end of this time, he left IBM and supported his family with his business. "I haven't received a paycheck from an employer for the past 15 years."

Dale says he was influenced by some of the greats like Zig Ziglar, Jim Rohn and others. But he gives the most credit to Jim Burke, Shaklee Master Coordinator. "He taught me that network marketing has nothing to do with products or how much a marketing plan pays. Network Marketing is about leadership development. The growth of your business is in direct proportion to the number of leaders you are able to develop."

Dale continues his remarks about Jim Burke, "I feel the man is light years ahead of this industry and that 99% of the people haven't figured out that we truly are in the 'Leadership development' business."

Dale has a long list of heroes. One of them is Pete Rose. "I grew up watching Pete play. I think he helped me understand at an early age to always give 110% and expect to win."

He credits his dad, Ben Calvert, for encouraging him with his patience, strength and constant support throughout his life. His other heroes are his Leadership team and all those "who have always believed in me."

The best thing about being self-employed for Dale Calvert is having the opportunity to share with other people how they can become debt-free, totally financially independent and gain one hundred percent control over their time.

He concludes, "Success is really only success when it can be shared and duplicated." ∎

David A. Nelson

Age: 53

Family: David & his wife Nanette have 3 sons & 1 daughter. Mark, 24 is a college graduate in business & a full-time network marketing professional; Scott, 22 has one year remaining to graduate from college; Dana, 17 is a Junior in High School & Craig, 16 is a sophomore.

Highest Education: MBA in Business Administration

Year started business: Started network marketing in 1988. Operated other businesses prior to that.

Type of business: Network marketing – teaching people how to make money.

Market: Those who desire to make money. It doesn't matter if they have money or don't have money, if they want to make money, they are the market.

Number of employees: 0

Best month (gross revenues): $40,000

Hours worked per week during start-up: 60-70

Hours worked per week now: 50-90 depending on meeting schedules, conference calls and writing.

Favorite business magazines: *Fast Company, Cutting Edge Opportunities, Personal Excellence*

Favorite business books and authors: *The Seven Habits of Highly Effective*

People by Stephen Covey, *You Were Born Rich* by Bob Proctor, *Think & Grow Rich* by Napoleon Hill.

Relaxes by: Reading, playing racquetball, going to movies, watching Sports Center, doing "stuff" with his kids, listening to inspirational tapes.

Keeps in shape physically by: Racquetball & basketball, sit-ups & weight lifting.

Favorite part of job: Teaching the opportunities of network marketing.

Least favorite part of job: Accounting & reporting requirements associated with a business.

Companies admired: ForMor International; Cutting Edge Media; Proctor & Gamble.

Favorite Quotes:

"The key to unlocking my potential is within me. It is in the power of my thought, my vision and my commitment." (Unknown)

"Give a man a fish and you feed him for a day...but teach him how to fish and you feed him for a lifetime" (A Wise Man)

"A year from now you may wish you had started today." (Karen Lamb)

David Nelson (center), vacationing with his kids

TOP PERFORMER
BY JAN WALLEN

Top performer is an apt description for **David Nelson.** He began in Corporate America where he was a top performer in the securities training industry, and is now the top money earner in his network marketing business.

David chose to leave Corporate America after becoming discouraged over "the politics and lies." He then worked with other entrepreneurs in small businesses. He describes this experience as successful but frustrating. The logical course was to strike out on his own, and twenty years ago he did just that. He has been in Network Marketing for eleven years. He began to earn a profit after approximately twelve months in the industry.

He says his parents had the greatest influence in his life by what they taught him through word and example. David has several heroes. He names Jesus as a hero for the teachings, the perfect example, and the outlook of the future.

Another hero is Michael Jordan due to his discipline and commitment to excellence and teamwork. He also admires eagles because they are the symbol of visionary leadership.

One award that has great meaning for David is his company's Crusader Award. He was the first one to receive it, and it has subsequently been named The David Nelson Crusader Award.

David writes articles each month for Cutting Edge Media publications. He has also produced several audio cassette tapes and training materials.

When asked what was the best thing about being in business for himself, David replied, "I like the freedom, flexibility, and the unlimited potential to obtain the rewards of my personal efforts in many areas of life."

David Nelson is the personification of what a Top Performer can achieve. ■

Scott Ohlgren

Age: 42

Family: Wife Gael, 51; Dog Bo, 3.

Highest Education: 1 semester of UWMadison

Year started business: 1989

Type of business: Marketer and National Trainer for Cell Tech, the superfood company.

Market: Children & adults wanting the next level of health & same people who want a home-based business.

Number of employees: 0

Best month (gross revenues): $53,000.

Hours worked per week during start-up: 70

Hours worked per week now: 60

Favorite business magazines: *Upline, Inc., Macworld*

Favorite business books and authors: *Awakening the Giant Within; Unlimited Power; The tape series, PowerTalks, all by Tony Robbins.*

Relaxes by: Paragliding, running on the beach, reading.

Keeps in shape physically by: Running & weight lifting.

Favorite part of job: Watching people step up & beyond their fear of greatness.

Least favorite part of job: Seeing people I love quit.

Companies admired: Apple Computer, Franklin Covey, Robbins Research

Favorite quotes:

"Success is 99% failure." (Soichiro Honda)

"Those who can't laugh hard at themselves leave the job to others." (Anonymous)

"Focus on where you want to go. Not on what you fear." (Anonymous)

The Face In The Mirror
BY JAN WALLEN

Scott Ohlgren ended up in business for himself because "I need to have the person I saw in the mirror each morning be the boss!"

He says that Anthony Robbins, peak performance coach, has had the most influence in his life. His hero is Daryl Kollman, Harvard scientist who was the first person to assay and study super blue-green algae.

It took him only six months to begin making a profit, and he says that the best thing about being his own boss in no wage! One of his proudest achievements was making the pages of the October, 1998, issue of Success Magazine.

Scott is the author of 3 Phase Manual, which has sold over 80,000 copies. He also created the video How to Develop a Prosperity Mind. You can order Scott's book and/or tape by calling 1-800-797-3912.

Through Network Marketing Scott Ohlgren has achieved his dream of having as his boss, the person he sees in the mirror each morning. ■

Jim Strickland

Age: "Same as Jack Benny! (39 & holding)"

Family: Wife, Jane B. Strickland. Son, Patrick O'Brien Strickland, 11.

Highest Education: Graduated from college with a business degree & worked on an MBA. Presently studying to become a naturopathic physician.

Year started business: 1979, started his own specialty chemical company, All American Chemicals, Inc. 1982, started as a distributor for Cambridge International.

Type of business: Has been in Network Marketing virtually full-time for the last 16 years...mainly in Nutrition & weight loss supplements.

Market: Our market is "aimed" at the "Baby Boomer" Generation and beyond! However, our products are really for anyone who wants to attain optimum health & financial independence.

Number of employees: 5

Best month (gross revenues): Sold $3 million in one month (wholesale)

Hours worked per week during start-up: 18 hours a day, 6 days a week.

Hours worked per week now: 60

Favorite business magazines: Success, Entrepreneur, Cutting Edge Opportunities

Favorite business books and authors: *Who Stole the American Dream* by

Burke Hedges; *Think & Grow Rich!* by Napoleon Hill, *Positive Living* by Dr. Robert Schuller.

Relaxes by: Reading positive, self-help books & listening to motivational self-help audios.

Keeps in shape physically by: Working out 5-6 days per week; resistance training 3 days per week.

Favorite part of job: The power of Network Marketing and watching people grow mentally, spiritually, physically & financially.

Least favorite part of job: Wasting time with MLM "junkies" who "bounce" from program to program.

Companies admired: "I admire Amway for their perseverance to fight the FTC and win for all of us! I also truly admire Harley-Davidson Motorcycles Company's triumphant turnaround to become an American icon and a great American success story."

Favorite quotes:

"Give enough people what they want and they will give you what you want!" (Zig Ziglar)

"As a man thinketh in his heart, so is he!" (The Holy Bible)

"I would rather earn 1% of 100 people's efforts than 100% of my efforts alone!" (J. Paul Getty)

Life-Long Entrepreneur Makes It Big In Network Marketing

BY JAN WALLEN

Jim Strickland began in business for himself when he was only twelve years old. He ran a paper route and then sub-contracted several other boys to help him deliver papers. When he was fourteen, he began a lawn cutting business and again ended up hiring several other boys to cut grass while he sold new customers.

Jim says, "I have been an entrepreneur virtually all of my life, except for a short time as an employee and two years in the U.S. Army Special Forces."

Geometric progression can be seen most vividly in Jim's income with Phoenix International. He began in October by making $485; jumped to $4100 in November and ended that year with $5995 for December. He got the new year off to a rousing start by earning $26,000; his March check was for $107,787 and May brought him $306,000.

The power of geometric growth is very real in Jim Strickland's life.

Jim say he has been most influenced by Jesus Christ. His heroes are Dr. Robert Schuller, a pastor; Zig Ziglar, a motivational speaker and trainer; and Lt. Colonel James "Bo" Gritz, the most highly decorated Green Beret commander in Viet Nam.

Along the way, Jim has received many honors. He was featured in Money Magazine in 1987 and was also named as one of the Outstanding Young Men in America in the same year. In addition, he has been featured in several network marketing and income opportunity magazines including, Networking for Success, Money N Profits, and Money Maker's Monthly.

He has been a top producer with Eagle Shield, Phoenix International, and Uniquest International.

Jim says, "I love being my own boss, working my own hours, and being in control of my own destiny."

He has recorded several audio tapes and videotapes. Currently he is working on a book on Network Marketing. His tapes may be purchased from Strickland Family Corp., PO Box 695, Destin, FL 3240-0695 or via fax at 1-850-654-7049.

From a paper route at age twelve to a six figure monthly income years later, Jim Strickland truly has the spirit of an entrepreneur. ∎

The Interviews

Chuck Branham
(CB)

Robert Butwin
(RB)

Dale Calvert
(DC)

David A. Nelson
(DN)

Scott Ohlgren
(SO)

Jim Strickland
(JS)

I'm starting a home business next month. I have a maximum of $3000 in start-up capital. Where should I invest it?

CB: Twenty-five hundred dollars in products to use, show, and sell, and five hundred dollars in tools, such as books, tapes, and videos.

RB: In marketing. In ways to get customers. It varies from company to company.

You want to use your start-up capital in building a customer base. This is more important than putting money in product. Invest in tools which will bring customers.

DC: Follow the suggestions of a successful, ethical upline. I would spend about $500 for an initial supply of products, training materials, and business aides. You must have a product that you can take to the market place and generate immediate retail sales. From this point on only use profits for advertising. Always invest a portion of your monthly profits in personal development programs, at least 10%. You never ask what it costs, only what is it worth?

DN: Take approximately $1,000 to establish an appropriate office: necessary files, day planner, telephone, business cards, fax machine, and some basic supplies from the network marketing company and distributor support group. Budget the remaining $2,000 over the next six months for the expenses of doing the business. Appropriate energy and time commitment with this "seed" money and the bonus money that is generated should create a viable business in six months time, and the cash flow to continue.

SO: Whoa. The first question is, what is the thing you love to do? If you're not loving what you do, if you don't love the basic industry you're in (in my case, the health field), you won't make it. Period. You must be so driven by a vision that it literally keeps you up at night, and wakes you in the morning. Period.

JS: I recommend "investing in yourself." I use DMS's (Dynamic Marketing Systems) Postcard Recruiting System for Nature's Gold. The cost is only $100.00 for 1000 glossy 3-color postcards with my own ID# on it. Then the cost to mail 1,000 postcards is only $200.00.

DMS handles the "follow-up" packages and sponsors the people who respond under me. I would also purchase a good mailing list, preferably 1,000 names with phone numbers from Cutting Edge Opportunities (cost =$250). The list must be good for the direct mail piece to work!

I would invest $200-$300 minimum in a good, plain paper fax machine. I would also run small classified ads "targeted" in the Business Opportunity section of the newspaper ($50/week max.). I would call my local phone company, set up "3 way" calling and a voice mail with them.

Also, I would purchase at least $200.00 in products from my company to use myself and show to others (and go on Monthly Auto Ship Plan). Next, I would go "online" and set up a custom Web page and submit it to all search engines, links, banner displays, etc. that "fit" my company and products.

Sales aids including product brochures, audiotapes, videos, etc...are very powerful when used properly! By working with my sponsor and/or upline I would find out what's working best to "duplicate" the company's "system."

I've just started a home business. My spouse has given me six months to make it work. Any advice?

CB: AOMA. All out massive action. Talk to lots of people with excitement and enthusiasm.

RB: The beauty of this business is that there is no time limit. Just keep developing the belief systems which will be your "passion to action." You will need to have consistent actions which will allow you to accomplish your objectives.

DC: First you must be real clear on what your spouse's definition of making it work means. If it is $500 per month profit and you are teachable that won't be a problem. If it is $5,000 a month, we will need a little longer than six months to get that done. We have a fantastic audio tape entitled "The Skeptical Spouse Syndrome", we also have a video from our Satellite Training entitled "Former Negative Husbands & Wife's Speak out", I would personally call your spouse and try to have him or her commit to watching the video and listening to the cassette. I would then follow up, take their pulse and just try to encourage them to be neutral until we can get your business off the ground. As I have said many times, we all have to deal with negative influences in our life, unfortunately some of us are sleeping with them. Thank goodness for me, my wife Stephanie has always been not only supportive, but active in our business.

DN: Make sure to do cash flow projections to verify that you can develop a positive cash flow in the business of choice. Associate with proven mentors who can guide you in the development of your personal knowledge and skills. Establish written goals and a plan of action. Make the time that you allocate for doing the business "sacred." In other words, it is a priority over which almost nothing takes precedence. Make sure you have a white-hot, burning desire in your chest for success and a total belief and commitment to what you are doing.

SO: Develop the attitude, "OK, I'll show her" and get busy. Get so proud of what you're doing, that you do not think/eat/do ANYTHING NOT RELATED TO YOUR DREAM.

JS: Go to work! If you want to make serious money, you just make a commitment! Work! Work! Work!

They say it takes money to make money. Should I try to get a small business loan for my start-up capital or just try to get by with my own limited finances?

CB: If I had several thousand dollars of my own, I'd use that. If not, I would borrow the money. When we started, we were broke so we borrowed the money. I was able to pay off the loan quickly and made over $100,000.00 the first full year.

RB: I don't recommend getting a loan, nor would I allow a short term financial situation to limit your growth in the business. There are always creative ways to find people who have money but no time who would like to have a profitable business. Before looking for that person, though, you must develop a strategy and be able to show them some level of success. So start where you are and make it work. You can build a great track record even in small steps.

DC: Absolutely Not. In network marketing $500 will get you up and going. Anyone who wants it bad enough can get their hands on $500. From that point on as long as you have a hot product that can be retailed, your profits should propel your business forward. My leadership team is full of people earning well over $100,000 a year who started their business with less than $500 and never put another nickel out of pocket expense into it. Unfortunately many people have tried to build a network marketing organization by throwing money at it, and that will never work.

DN: This depends upon the business and what your ultimate goal is. The beauty of network marketing is that people can get started part-time and usually don't have to go into debt to be successful in building a very profitable business.

SO: Get by on your own sweat. Make it work with what you've got.

JS: Work up a good budget for your business with your sponsor and then figure out if you will need a loan or can finance your business. Retailing product every day can produce daily PROFITS! You can "roll" these profits to make more money! A lot of your business can be "financed" via your credit cards initially and then be paid off as soon as commission checks come in!

Do you consider yourself an "early adopter" of new technology?

CB: I am not an early adapter of new technology but tend to wait until some of the early bugs are worked out.

RB: I'm not an early adopter but I recognize the value of technology and I don't resist it.

DC: Yes. However, I think many people have made the mistake of trying to build their network marketing business hiding behind computer screens, voice mail boxes, and fax machines. Network marketing is about relationships, always has been, always will be.

DN: No. I'm not really technically oriented. Remember, I like the relationships and the people. But I add technology to my business as I see it helping me and my people doing the business more effectively. I also have tremendous associates who assist dramatically in this area.

SO: No. I wait until it's stable (in the case of software), and useful. I wait to see others using it effectively.

JS: Yes! I am constantly searching for new, innovative ways to build my business faster!

What is the primary use for your toll-free line?

CB: The primary use of our toll-free line is to take orders for books, tapes, and videos.

DC: Lead Generation

DN: I utilize toll-free numbers for responses to my advertising. I don't use a toll-free number for people to call back and visit personally.

JS: I use toll-free order lines, toll-free fax order lines and even toll-free pagers and presentation lines.

Describe your computer system:

RB: I have an IBM Pentium machine and a scanner. I use ACT data base for contact management. I'm planning to get a Website up this year

DC: My #1 Computer is a Toshiba Infinia with large 20" monitor. I also use 3 others, one being an IBM laptop that I take on the road and use for presentations among other things. We also use a flatbed scanner, digital camera, 2 color printers, and one laser jet printer.

DN: I have three or four Macs of different capacity that we use at various locations in our homebased office. A laser printer is a must. I have access to a scanner that meets my needs.

SO: Mac 8.1 OS. Powerbook G3, 233mhz, 164 RAM. I also use a printer and scanner.

What software do you consider in the "must-have" category?

CB: Microsoft Publisher, for newsletters and flyers.

DC: I think it depends on what people are comfortable with. I use, Eudora for Email, Quicken, Word, Ascend for a contact manager, & My Mailing List for some of our direct mail programs.

DN: It's a must to have a good word processing program. For me, it's also a must to have a contact management program.

SO: Word 98, Quark, Now Contact.

JS: QuickBooks

What other technologies, if any, do you use in your business?

CB: I use a cellullor phone and a pager.

Technology Utilized

	Fax*	Fax-on-Demand	Toll-Free	Voice Mail	Computer	Email	Internet	Website	Email Auto-Responders
Chuck Branham	✓		✓	✓	✓	✓	✓	✓	
Robert Butwin	✓			✓	✓	✓	✓		
Dale Calvert	✓	✓	✓	✓	✓	✓	✓	✓	✓
David Nelson	✓	✓	✓	✓	✓	✓	✓	✓	
Scott Ohlgren	✓	✓		✓	✓	✓	✓	✓	
Jim Strickland	✓	✓	✓	✓	✓	✓	✓		✓

* Dedicated fax line

RB: I use cell phones and palmtops. I also use a high res projector and Power Point for presentations. I think you can make exciting information look even more attractive when you put things together with care.

DC: Cell phone, palm size tape recorder.

DN: I don't use a cell phone in my business because when I am away from the phone, I really want to be away. I am on the phone a great deal each week and there are times to get away. I use my computers when I am in my office. I'm more efficient with them on that basis. I always have something with me to read when I am out and about and find that provides great personal energy, information, and support.

SO: Hands-free cell phone, headset at office, copy machine.

JS: Cellular phones, pagers.

If you use the World Wide Web, name up to five personal favorite business URL's our readers can benefit from:

DC: www.mlmhelp.com, www.upline.com, www.mlmers.com, www.mlm.com, www.newimageint.com

DN: www.discovermoney.com

JS: www.fireyourboss.com; www.naturesgold.com; www.emeraldcoast.com

Of all the technology you use, rank the top three:

CB: Of all the technology I use, the top three are 1. telephone, 2. Fax, 3. computer (actually my wife uses the computer).

RB: Cell phones and The Palm Pilot are my favorite.

DC: Phone, Conference Calling, Computer

DN: Telephone, Computer, Fax

SO: Fax machine, VoiceMail, Conference Calling.

JS: Computers; Fax Machines; Cellular Phones

Do you market on the Internet?

CB: I don't presently market on the internet.

RB: Not yet. But am planning to.

DC: I believe the only reason to advertise in the cold market is too support the warm market recruiting efforts of your future leaders. Yes I advertise on the

Internet, but this is a warm market business. We place print advertising to drive people to our Web site(s). Also we are starting to include our Web address on virtually everything that is mailed from this office. Some of our newer audio tapes refer people back to our Website. Approximately 20% of our leads are generated through the Web.

DN: Yes, we have a Website on the Internet. Our support organization provides a Website that distributors can use in their marketing efforts. At this time, I don't personally use the Internet to generate significant leads. Less than 10% of sales come from this method of marketing.

SO: No

JS: Yes. I use several links, Websites, email, etc. 10% of my sales come from this method of marketing.

Do you use direct mail?

CB: I use direct mail a little now and then to send tapes and literature to prospects. A small percentage of our business comes from this.

RB: Yes. Mass marketing by mailing to targeting lists. Over 80% of my sales come from direct mail. I spend my money to test what we do so that the people I am working with who also use direct mail will get the best results.

DC: Yes, but this is a warm market business. We have several different recruiting programs that generate leads through direct mail. We mail out 3 different postcards offering 3 different audio tapes as well as a 7-step advertising campaign for our generic mlm training course "Confessions of a Network Marketing Millionaire". Approximately 10% of our leads come from direct mail.

DN: Yes, some direct mail is used. It is used to generate leads and to follow-up with certain "suspects" that have been recognized through various lead generation sources. Less than 10% of sales come from this method of marketing.

SO: No

JS: Yes. We mail postcards using DMS (Robt Martz). His powerful Postcard Recruiting System accounts for 25% of my sales.

Do you use print media?

CB: Yes. I do some classified newspaper advertising primarily to prospect for distributors and have had some good results from this.

RB: Yes. I have done display ads and classified ads. Once I put the following ad in the Business Opportunity section of several major entrepreneurial magazines. "Robert Butwin Goes Crazy and Offers His Million Dollar Success Secrets for Free!" I got phenomenal response. The key to using print media is to make sure you have the right headline for the right audience. That's what's going to get people to want to find out more.

DC: Yes, but again, this is a warm market business. We run classified ads as well as full page advertisements in network marketing publications. We also have customized recruiting programs that we use in local markets throughout the United States and Canada. Some of our customized recruiting programs focus on stay at home mothers, chiropractors, and small business owners. We have specific ads, follow up information, and audio recruiting cassettes designed specifically for these markets as well as others. Approximately 25% of our leads come from print media.

DN: I use magazine print media advertising extensively. I promote the name of my network marketing company distributor support organization, and generate leads from print media advertising. At this point in my network marketing career, approximately 70% of my leads come from advertising, but that's not the way it was when I first came into the business.

SO: No.

JS: Yes. Magazines, newspapers, etc. I run classifieds, display ads, card decks, etc. It accounts for 10% of my sales.

Do you use radio and/or TV advertising?

CB: I don't use radio or TV advertising because I doubt it would be cost effective.

RB: No

DC: Yes, TV shows. New Image International has produced a powerful 30-minute infomercial that distributors can run in their local markets to generate leads for both our products and business opportunity. We believe very much in the concept of "TARGETED" cold market recruiting. We only recruit in the cold market to support the warm market recruiting efforts of future leaders within that town. The TV show allows myself and my leaders to focus in on a specific city where we have an up and coming leader. We run the TV shows, work the leads, and build one solid line under our up and coming leader while supporting them with 3-way calls etc. within their warm market. TV shows generate approximately 30% of our leads.

DN: I am personally not using radio or TV advertising.

SO: No.

JS: Yes. I use Morning shows as a guest talking about nutrition, "cutting edge" supplements, etc. This generates 5% of my sales.

What other kinds of marketing do you utilize?

CB: I belong to a barter club that gets me in front of some prospects. I have belonged to two leads clubs that have resulted in some business. I utilize booths at trade shows and fairs occasionally.

RB: Person to person is the most cost effective form of marketing. I meet people constantly. My first focus is to develop a relationship with them. Within a relationship it's very natural to involve them in my business in some way.

DC: Approximately 80% of the distributors that join our organization are satisfied retail customers first – imagine that! We teach a specific system for converting retail customers to distributors. All cold market advertising is used only to get into someone's warm market. We also use Trade Shows, Fairs, Fax Blast, Video Tape Recruiting, Drop Cards, Product Brochures, Mini-Billboards, Car Signs, Car SunShades, Bumper Stickers, Bulletin Board tear off Flyers, Product promotional Displays in small businesses, and many more programs to create massive retail sales and ultimately new distributors. We teach specific step by step methods for all our recruiting and retail activities. Our philosophy is you retail to recruit.

DN: Obviously, personal networking is a means of marketing that is critical in my business. I am always trying to get referrals from people because of the strength of referral marketing.

SO: Community outreach/talks.

JS: "3 way" calling.

Do you recommend using a toll-free number in advertising?

CB: So far, I haven't used a toll-free number much in our Nikken business. If people are really interested they are willing to pay for the call.

RB: No.

DC: Yes and No. If I am opening up a new area with a new recruit and I want massive action and the phone ringing off the hook then yes we use a toll-free number. Once a distributor is off to a fast start we get much more selective about who we talk to, and who we will recruit, we really don't want 80% of the people that respond to our advertising campaigns! At this time we will let the prospects start paying for the call, the serious ones will.

DN: Yes, I recommend the use of toll-free numbers because it increases the likelihood of someone responding to an ad. You have to make it easy for people to respond.

JS: Yes! Increases response!

Where do you market?

CB: I market primarily in our local area but more and more nationally and internationally.

RB: All geographic markets.

DC: Presently we are building our business in targeted areas throughout the United States and Canada; however, my generic mlm training program "Confessions of a Network Marketing Millionaire" is being sold around the world.

DN: At this time, I focus my marketing efforts nationally. It's a huge market.

SO: Locally

JS: I market internationally through the Internet and market nationwide with "3 way" calling, ads., etc.

THE HOME OFFICE:

How should someone set up their home office to maximize its effectiveness?

CB: At our home, which is paid for by Nikken, Inc on a special home bonus, my wife has her office at one end of the house and I have my office at the other end of the house on a different level. Our house is fairly large with twelve telephones and six bathrooms. This gives us flexability. A place for everything and everything in its place is a good goal.

RB: No special tips.

DC: It should be comfortable and motivational with pictures reminding you of WHY you are doing your business. It should be in a separate room in your home with as much privacy as possible.

DN: The most effective home office is obviously private. It's critical to project the professional image even and especially when working in a home-based business. It also provides a place for better concentration of effort and effectiveness. My office is a working office. It's not for show, therefore, the desks, tables, computers, fax machines, phones, copy machine, etc. are situated for efficient and serious use. When doing business from home, it's critical to have separate phone lines. A home-based business is really an important business, so people must treat it like a serious business.

SO: All within reach. Also, get a phone headset.

JS: Organize in one room if possible.

Are there any ground rules you've established for yourself, family, etc. for operating at home successfully?

CB: I try to give my wife and those who work for us privacy so they and I can concentrate on what we are focused on doing. I take brief rest breaks during the day so I keep fresh and energized.

RB: We always take Sunday off. I do keep regular hours. I'm usually in the office in the morning. I have a place in my home which is set aside as my office. I keep it separate from where my family life takes place.

DC: Only one. When dad gives the cut throat sign they know to quiet it down NOW! My daughters have never known anything except dad has an office at home. They don't remember me ever working at IBM. My best advice is to take time for bedtime stories, and communicating with your family.

DN: My wife and kids know the times that it's critical to give me the privacy and quiet that I need. However, because I'm in business for myself, they also know of the flexibility and we try to maximize that for the family and family things. Like in other careers and businesses there is give and take and rules and guidelines must be established. It takes a certain amount of discipline on their part and my part to make it work.

JS: Set regular hours.

Do you consider working at home an advantage or disadvantage to your business overall?

CB: I very much consider working at home an advantage to my business because it eliminates fighting traffic and is much less stressful.

RB: It's a great advantage. I don't have to commute. I have everything I need at my finger tips. Working at home makes my time feel like my time. Work is a natural extension of all the things I do. Working at home makes this really easy.

DC: A definite advantage. I love talking on the phone, doing business while sitting on the deck looking out over the lake in our backyard or on a raft floating in the swimming pool.

DN: Working a homebased business is a huge advantage. There are tax advantages. There are relationship advantages. There are no-commute advantages. I know that sometimes, Nanette, my wife, would like to have more separation, but she also realizes and appreciates the benefits. A significant benefit to her is that I'm much happier.

SO: ADVANTAGE!

JS: There is a wonderful advantage to having a "home based" business.

Do you farm out any of your work?

CB: I farm out parts of my work. I delegate some of the routine things, and things I don't enjoy, to our employees, such as duplication of tapes, mailing out our newsletters, etc. I like to concentrate on the high priority things I do best, such as prospecting, follow up, presenting the business opportunity and doing 3 way phone calls with team members.

RB: No

DC: Yes, as much as possible. All the printing, audio, video duplication, packaging, etc. is farmed out. My staff does everything else. I delegate as much as possible. I concentrate on developing relationships with my people. The training leadership and direction of the organization is where I attempt to concentrate my efforts. People don't care how much you know until they know how much you care. I understand completely that my success is in direct proportion to the number of people I can inspire to become leaders.

DN: Very little of my work is sent out to others. Most of it can't be delegated because of the high-touch relationships that are developed. With expanding organizations and need for support systems, some of that function eventually must be done by others. Some personal contacting can never be done by others. However, leaders must be developed and in order to assist them in developing the knowledge, skills, and techniques, it's critical to delegate important functions of business-building activity. It's always difficult to delegate issues that relate to expense control and the handling of money resources. One must be very careful as it's a matter of trust!

SO: I farm out as much as possible! I farm out my taxes to someone who keeps them below 10%, my printing, my design, everything I can afford to farm out, I farm out.

JS: Yes. I farm out printing, fulfillment, etc.

Do you encourage or discourage partnerships?

CB: I discourage partnerships.

RB: I don't encourage partnerships.

DC: Discourage, having witnessed too many problems first hand.

DN: I discourage partnerships as they usually don't work out in the long run. It takes a very synergistic relationship to have partnerships work in the long run. Most of the time it's the money and/or the ego that busts up the partnership. Or perhaps it's the work ethic issue. It is difficult to match up energy and work ethic of the partners. At some point in time a partner is satisfied with the rewards and wants to slow down. Then, the challenge is to fairly accommodate the future work and rewards that occur.

JS: Discourage

Do you encourage or discourage hiring family members?

CB: We have made hiring family members work pretty well.

RB: There's nothing wrong with it. My kids actually have helped me do mailings. It teaches them responsibility and earning money at an early age. It's also something we do together.

DC: Encourage, they tend to be very loyal and trustworthy. I also create special projects such as envelope stuffing etc. for our church youth group to help them raise money. A youth group can knock out a direct mail project in no time.

DN: Family members should be hired with appropriate guidelines and expectations. There should be "no free lunch." When they are productive and proactive, sure hire them. Here's a warning that I just picked up in my reading: Be very careful about hiring "in-laws." It can be devastating.

JS: Encourage.

When legal issues arise, what's your usual response?

CB: When legal issues arise, we can have our daughter, Terry, who works for us, give an opinion because she is a paralegal. Also, we have an attorney who handles our legal matters.

RB: I check with a lawyer.

DC: Fight! Fortunately only a couple of issues have come up in the past 18 years. I have learned it is not worth the time, energy and emotion for me to get involved. I let my lawyers handle it.

DN: Be careful. Be patient and get a good understanding of what the real issues are before deciding on a course of action. We must protect our assets and business. I never wish to seek revenge. It's a negative thing and is far too prominent in the world today. There's also way too much "legal stuff."

JS: I try to evaluate the issue first. If I can work it out, I do. If not, I contact an attorney as a last resort.

Does earning a lot of money improve the quality of your life, and if so, in what ways?

CB: Having a lot of money definitely has improved the quality of my life. I am now able to travel, go on cruises, hire things done that I don't want to do and purchase many things such as cameras, a home theater, etc.

RB: You're able to live more fully. The biggest advantage of high earnings is that it gives you time to make a difference with other people. When you're under time pressure, it's hard to really give of yourself. That takes time. When you can invest time in someone though, and see them grow, that's a pleasure which I wouldn't want to do without.

DC: Yes, I have had it and not had it, and it is better to have it! Money just makes you more of what you already are. If you are a giving person, you will simply have the privilege of giving more after you have the money. It has enabled us to support some very worthwhile causes, do more for our church, and our community. I personally believe that it is a SIN to be poor. When you have money you don't have to physically be there to support your fellow man. Personally it is very gratifying to be able to provide the finer things in life for our children. I like going into a fine restaurant and not even looking at the prices on the menu. It is also nice to be able to take off to Cancun or Aruba whenever you feel like it.

DN: There's two issues here. One is quality of life and the other is lifestyle.

Earning a lot of money obviously can increase lifestyle, but in the process lowers quality of life. A lot of money is not required for people to enjoy a quality of life. In fact, some of the most quality years of my life were those days at the university and just after when Nanette and I didn't have a lot of money. We had plenty for our needs and enjoyed many things, but a lot of money we did not have. As most people know, all too frequently a lot of money really changes people into greedy, selfish, self-centered people. It's critical that we remember to love people and use money. Contributing one's time in the service of others, as well as money, certainly helps people keep the appropriate focus on quality life and on being a quality person. Not just the money, but time in service of others.

SO: Money was the missing key to my life. Having worked for a wage all my life, I was always broke. Imagine not worrying about money. The person who said that money can't buy you happiness should be found and shot. Well, it actually can't buy you happiness, but it buys something awfully close.

JS: Yes! It means I can provide good education for my child, dental, health insurance, clothing, vacations, etc.

Best general tax advice?

CB: The best general tax advice I can give is keep real good records and hire a good CPA.

RB: Basically, you are able to write off many things if you do this business properly.

DC: I have heard all my life that rich people don't pay taxes; that isn't true. Find a good accountant, and educate yourself as much as possible.

DN: The best general tax advice that I can give is: recordkeeping, recordkeeping, recordkeeping is the key activity.

SO: Tax advice: don't do it yourself!! And if you can't find someone who teaches you how to keep it below 15%, get someone else.

JS: Hire a very competent CPA; get references from business people who are successful.

Best general investment advice?

CB: The best investment advice I would give is to invest in yourself. Invest in great books, tapes and videos and seminars. Also, invest in your own business.

RB: Invest in yourself and your business is your best investment   I put 30% of my profits back into my business each year. I also invest in personal growth. I don't hesitate to attend seminars and read books which may give me new insights about this business or about myself.

DN: Make certain that your investments are not so risky that you lose your principle. Once you have earned the money, please, make sure that you preserve it. Many people have made the money, but they don't retain it. Another critical practice is to always set aside 10% of your earnings for investment.

JS: Invest in yourself! Training in MLM or whatever your chosen field is.

*You're in business already, and you've just received a windfall of $20,000.
What would you do with it?*

CB: If I received a windfall of $20,000.00 I would give a tithe (10%) to our church and probably use the rest to pay on loans to move us toward our goal of being debt free.

RB: I would use it to match the funds of other key leaders in my group.

DC: Give $5,000 to our church and put $5,000 in each of my three daughters investment accounts.

DN: A windfall of $20,000 that would come to me would be invested into my retirement account!

SO: Lower debt, or invest in low risk stocks.

JS: Reinvest 70% back into my business into advertising, printing, etc. Retain the other 30% for "cash flow."

What do you lead with – your company's products or the business opportunity?

CB: I generally lead with my company's business opportunity but the products are very important and I do cover them in my presentations.

RB: In mass marketing activities, I lead with product. When I meet someone in life, I lead with the business opportunity.

DC: I don't feel leading with one or the other is correct so we teach both. We have a specific step by step, word by word, unified system for retailing which ultimately exposes the business to our retail customers. Eighty percent of our distributors are satisfied retail customers first. We also teach a specific step by step process leading with the Business. It includes a video tape, and 3-way call- weekly business briefing.

DN: I am in the business of teaching people how to make money. I lead with the business opportunity. Most legitimate network marketing companies have great products. They must if they want us to go market them on a referral basis. Most part-time people don't make money in network marketing because they don't understand the principles of the business of network marketing, which is making profits, making money, and don't get into a program designed for part-timers.

SO: Lead with products.

JS: I lead with both! I am looking for people who want optimum health and financial freedom, not just product users!

Rank the following traits in order of their importance in building a successful network marketing business: enthusiasm, persistence, knowledge, communication skills.

CB: 1. enthusiasm, 2. persistence, 3. knowledge, 4. communication skills.

RB: Knowledge & Communications skills are a tie for my top two. You're sending and receiving messages constantly. You have to send and receive the right messages. Knowledge is important because if you really understand what this business is all about you'll be able to package it properly. Communications skills are important because ultimately, this business is about your relationships with people. Good relationships always start with communications. Persistence and enthusiasm follow.

DC: Persistence, Communication Skills, Enthusiasm, Knowledge

DN: Enthusiasm, Knowledge, Persistence, Communication Skills

SO: Communication Skills, Enthusiasm (really, belief), Persistence, Knowledge.

JS: Enthusiasm, communication skills, knowledge and persistence.

How long were you in network marketing before you saw your first four-figure commission check? Five-figure check?

CB: I was in my current network marketing company three months before I saw my first four figure commission check and seven months before I saw my first five figure check.

RB: My first four figure check came after two years. My first five figure check after five years.

DC: Four Figure in 4 Months, Five Figure in 2 Years

DN: Four figures, approximately 18 months, Five figures, approximately 24 months

SO: 4 figures: 9 months; 5 figures: 4 years.

JS: 3 months to $3,000+ per month; 6 months to $10,000+ per month.

What's more important – the initial contact with a prospect or the follow-up?

CB: I think the initial contact with a prospect is very important, but in many cases the follow up is even more important.

RB: They're both equally important. You have to make a good first impression to get their involvement. If you don't follow up properly, they'll slip between the cracks.

DC: We teach that you need a minimum of 40 contacts per month....... but if you don't follow up you are wasting you time! Follow up is more important than the initial contact!

DN: The initial contact is more important, because without an initial contact there will be no follow-up. Follow-up is the most frustrating part of network marketing because many times it's difficult to get in touch with people. Also, most networkers don't realize just how much follow-up and relationship building must be done in order to sponsor some really good people. Prospecting is probably the single most important activity in network marketing.

SO: Follow up.

JS: Follow up! The fortune is in the "follow up"!

You've just recruited a promising new distributor – how do you help them get off to a good start – or do you consider that the new distributor's responsibility?

CB: When I recruit a promising new distributor I get them on a proven system which is designed to give them a simple step by step method which will help them reach their goals. We provide complete support which helps them become strong and able to stand on their own two feet.

RB: I feed them the right information and I stay with them so that they can get a few wins under their belts. Ultimately, I never desert them because I'm always going to be there for ongoing advice. I am clear in communicating with all new distributors that I'm always available for support.

DC: We teach a specific step by step plan for getting our new people off to a good start. It is called the 72 hour action plan and it is basically designed to get them to $500 per month within their first 90 days. Our goal is to create so much activity and so much excitement that our new distributor has trouble sleeping at night. We have to create it –we certainly can't expect them to.

DN: A sponsor is different from a recruiter. Certainly there are sponsoring responsibilities. It's not just a privilege, it's an obligation. The most important thing that a sponsor can do for a new distributor is to securely involve them in the total turnkey system that is provided by the distributor support organization. While doing that, the sponsor not only creates trust and increases the strength of the relationship, but also fosters the duplication aspect of the business.

New distributors soon realize there are more resources than just the individual sponsor. New distributors realize that they don't have to reinvent the wheel. New distributors realize that there is "institutional" support available, not only for them, but for the distributors that they bring into the business. Tapping into the establish turnkey system is the most important activity.

JS: I teach them our system. a) Use the products; b) Wear the "attention getter" badge; c) Pass out free samples and brochures!; d) Talk to people! Don't "pre-judge" anyone!

How do you get your best leads?

CB: I get my best leads from acquaintances.

RB: Living life. The people I meet. Sometimes great leads come in unexpected ways. You have to be open when meeting people. You have to be open when doing anything in life.

DC: No question –from the Warm Market of the people I recruit!

DN: The best leads come from warm market and the expanded circle of interest of people. That's networking. Always has been and always will be! In going to the new/cold market, my best leads have come from print media advertising and from lead generations services that use print media advertising.

SO: Meeting new people.

JS: I get some of my best leads by meeting people at civic functions, church meetings, etc.

I'm planning a big local meeting. What's the best way to fill the room?

CB: These day if I am planning a big local meeting I would use flyers and our voice mail messaging system. I would make an announcement to our key team members in the local area so they could pass the word to their leaders and so on.

RB: No special tips.

DC: We currently have over 130 weekly opportunity meetings being held within our organization on a weekly basis, please believe me when I say.........you build your local group and then you fill the room. If you try to fill the room to build your local group, you will be trying ten years from now.

DN: The best way to fill the room for a network marketing meeting is to have a lot of distributors who are active in doing personal inviting. You must create the atmosphere of an impending event and make it special. Generate the enthusiasm among your people that they should invite people to come and encourage the new invitees to invite people.

JS: About two months before I do a meeting, I usually run ads in the city I "target" to work in. I try to find several "leaders" to work with first and then teach them to sponsor 5-10 people each. Then we invite all of these people our Nationwide Weekly Conference Calls to teach them our recruiting "system." If they follow our system, we will usually have 75-100 or more people in our meeting.

I need to generate a hundred leads within 60 days. What's my best strategy to achieve this?

CB: If I needed to generate a hundred leads within 60 days I would run several classified ads in the newspaper. I would also call people on my prospect list and would ask for referrals as well.

RB: Find a lead source (fax blast, or Ad-net or lists) or do a trade show. I've had a lot of success meeting people and developing leads at trade shows. The bigger question is how to package what you have and approach your leads.

DC: I would run our company infomercial. If I didn't have that available I would run a couple of "TARGETED" classifieds in my local paper and then blitz the town with drop cards, bulletin board flyers, mini billboards, etc. This business becomes easy when people realize they will never run out of people to talk to and start sorting instead of convincing.

DN: The best way to generate 100 leads is to evaluate the expanded circle of influence. Beyond that, going to the new/cold market, the best way is to tap into appropriate lead generation sources. I have a great relationship with a reliable source that is efficient, cost effective, and productive. It's part of our lead generation system and is a must for organizations to be successful in teaching and helping people go beyond their circles of influence.

JS: I purchase 1,000 "Hot" leads from Cutting Edge Opportunities magazine and mail postcards to them; then I follow up with a FREE booklet offer. Everyone wants FREE information. I have developed a booklet called The Insider's Special Report, "How To Creates a 6-Figure Income From the Comfort of your Home!"

How many distributors must a person recruit each month to succeed in network marketing?

CB: To succeed in Network Marketing I would recommend recruiting two to four each month for the first year and after that one or two each month.

RB: It's not a question of how many you recruit. It's what you do with the people you do recruit. Take time up front to understand what their expectations are. Know what they want and what they're willing to do. Then you can make decisions together about how to work with each other.

DC: We teach that you must get your skills and attitudes to a level where you can comfortably recruit 5 people a month. You do that until you have 5 serious students. If you and your 5 students each recruit 5 a month you will soon become a super star in this industry.

DN: In the appropriate program, a distributor can recruit one person every other month and be successful in network marketing. Obviously, to enhance the chances for success, one a month would be much better. Most people don't realize that it's the consistent and persistent activity of sponsoring one person a month that can make them financially stable, create a greater quality of life, and even a lifestyle.

JS: I believe in personally sponsoring one new Distributor every week and teaching them how to "do the same thing!" This builds excitement and it also builds checks fast!

Best tips for surviving rejection?

CB: The best tips for surviving rejection are: don't take it personally. Tell the prospect, "This may or may not be for you." Realize that rejection is not always final but may only be temporary.

RB: In some ways, because of the way I do my business, I don't feel that I have to face a lot of rejection. I usually try to pose questions to people which they would feel comfortable saying "yes" to.

If you develop a good rapport - a good relationship with someone and get to understand where they may be at regarding the business and feel that they are not ready to get involved directly at this time, I might ask them if I could ask a small favor. Since we've already established a relationship, they feel good about saying yes to this. Then I ask them if, when they come across people who may appreciate this kind of opportunity, they would pass along their name and number to me so that I may contact them, this feels like a request they're happy to help with.

DC: Get rejected over and over again until it doesn't phase you. I used every rejection to strengthen my resolve. Most people let fear of failure and fear of rejection in preventing them from the greatest opportunity in history. Develop strong reasons for doing this business and you will persist through all disappointment and rejection. Without strong reasons I can guarantee you failure! That is why we have ALL of our new distributors complete what we call a 20 Reasons sheet. Until you know why the how doesn't matter!

DN: The best tip for surviving rejection is the strong posture: "I reject people, people don't reject me." Nanette, my wife prefers that I teach it like this: "I always seek win-win relationships." That means that when you discover that the prospect doesn't like network marketing, and really means it, disqualify the prospect and move on. That certainly wouldn't create a win-win relationship. Ms. Stud puts it this way, "Say no first!" If a "suspect" is not willing to work to build a downline, but wants you to build it for him/her (this is clearly a welfare case), disqualify the prospect. That way the telephone never gets heavy because you are the rejector not the rejectee. Pretty strong posture, but it means that I don't deal with rejection. Of course, we must disqualify nicely. We are not trying to hurt people and make people feel badly.

JS: Think of sponsoring or selling as a "baseball game"! Think about it! If you sell or sponsor 3 out of every 10 serious "prospects," you will be hitting .300 just like in the "majors"! All "great" baseball players would love to average .300 or better! Remember the old saying, "S.W., S.W., S.W., S.W., Next!" "Some will, some will not, so what, someone's waiting, next!"

In Network Marketing, it's a "numbers" game! You're in the business of "sorting" - red apples - ("great" prospects), green apples - ("prospects" who need a little more "polish" and training and they could become "great" distributors) and bad (rotten) apples (those who you could never develop into leaders and are not worth wasting your time over).

Do you recommend that new distributors prospect close friends and family?

CB: I do recommend that new distributors prospect close friends and family. If you have something valuable you would want to offer it to those you love the most. In the beginning the new distributor's sponsor or other active upline usually goes along to present the products and income opportunity because they have more credibility and experience.

RB: Yes. This business is all about helping people succeed and working with people who you enjoy being with. It makes perfect sense to want to work with people who you already know and like and then to do what you can to help them live the lifestyle they aspire to.

DC: Yes! If you have found the greatest opportunity in the world, would you rather share it with people you love or strangers? People who have trouble going to their warm market do so for only two reasons.

#1. They have no belief in the company and opportunity themselves or...

#2. They are not value focused, they are full of greed. When you can learn to share this opportunity for what it will do for others, and get the dollar signs out of your eyes your business will explode!

It really is true you can have anything in life you want if you help enough other people get what they want! Your obligation is to expose the opportunity. It ends there. If they join great, if they don't great! Value Focused Professionals sort---Greedy, Selfish Amateurs try to Convince!

DN: Absolutely, it is a fundamental principle of network marketing theory. If folks are not willing to go to their warm market friends and family (warm market is a small part of one's bigger circle of influence), something is missing in the belief level. Network marketing is networking!

SO: Depends. Are they close friends/family? Supportive? Does the new distributor care too much about their family's opinion? If so, do like I did: talk with people you don't know, and don't know you.

JS: Absolutely! Never "prejudge" anyone! "Situations" change and people are motivated by different things that happen in their lives (i.e., they might get "laid off" from their job, they purchase a new car and need more money, etc). Friends and family are excellent prospects for your home-based business.

In five years I'll be....

CB: I will be earning several million dollars per year and giving lots of money to the causes we believe in.

RB: I'll probably be doing what I am now. I really enjoy this business. I feel very fortunate to have the opportunity to live well and to be able to make a difference in many people's lives.

DC: In five years I'll be doing what I am doing now because I love it!

DN: In five years, I'll be teaching more and more people in a much broader scope the awesome opportunity that is to be found in network marketing. In five years, more and more part-time people will actually be earning money in network marketing.

JS: In five years I'll be helping people of "all walks of life" exit the "Rat Race" forever, and achieve the true American Dream of optimum health and financial independence!

In ten years I'll be...

CB: In ten years, I'll be earning even more millions of dollars per year and giving even more money to the causes we believe in. I will have made many more friends and helped many thousands of people world wide with our products and business opportunity.

RB: I'll still probably be doing the same thing, though I hope that after ten years, I will have been able to help more people get on track to realize their dreams.

DC: In ten years I will be known as part of a group of people that are in the process of rewriting network marketing history by returning it to its roots of personal development and empowering others to become all they can become.

DN: In ten years, I'll be more excited than ever about network marketing because the image of the industry will be changed and changing. Because of revolutionary Wave 4™ compensation plans, part-time people will be earning money and the general population will become aware of this critical fact.

JS: In ten years, I'll be still doing the same thing! I'll also continue working with a "dream team" of research scientists and product formulators to help develop "cutting edge" anti-aging nutraceutical health products.

What most motivates you in building your business?
CB: What most motivates me in building my business is the belief that I am doing God's will for me in helping many folks with our products and our business opportunity. Also, I love making new friends.

RB: Helping other people realize that the course they're on is not going to help them realize what they want in life, then helping them get on track.

Getting what you want has to be more than trading time for a wage (as people do in corporate jobs) or buying a job (like many people do when they buy a business).

Helping people become what they can be – to reach their potential and live the way they want to live – is the greatest motivation for me to do what I do.

DC: Helping others obtain their FREEDOM!

DN: Make no mistake about it, I love the money. But beyond money and a driving force which motivates me is the cause, the crusade of altering the reputation of network marketing by enabling part-time networkers to make money. If the industry is to achieve the greatness that is projected, the part-timers must make money. Without that happening, the industry will not become truly great. That crusade motivates me!

SO: Transforming the perception of How Health Works. Of becoming the 7 Habits of Highly Healthy People.

JS: I stay motivated 24 hours a day, 7 days a week! I love setting goals - short range, medium range and long range goals and accomplishing these goals! I love watching people succeed too! This motivates me even more!

How often do you read books and/or listen to or watch tapes for improving your business skills or knowledge?
CB: I read books, listen to audio tapes and watch videos on a daily basis for the purpose of improving my business skills and knowledge. I passionately believe in the use of great books, tapes, and videos for personal development and for introducing a business opportunity to people.

Because I feel so strongly about the benefits of these tools, I started a business called Success Express, Inc located at 3844 So. Pine St. suite B, Tacoma, WA 98409. The phone number is 800-966-8887 to order a free catalog. We donate 100% of the net profit from this business to several charities that help under-privileged children.

RB: I listen to tapes daily and read books often as well.

DC: Daily. Everyday for the past 18 years without exception.....it is the most vital part of my success.

DN: I am involved in personal self-development on a daily basis for a minimum of 45 minutes, often more than that (this is not the physical type, but the professional, emotional, and spiritual personal development).

SO: Virtually every, single day. As in 360 days a year.

JS: I do it daily! Nearly everyday of my life! Art Williams, Tommy Hopkins, Les Brown, Zig Ziglar, Anthony Robbins...they are all favorites!

The most underrated activity in business is?
CB: The most underated activitiy in business is prayer.

RB: Personal growth and development. As I reflect back on how I've accomplished what I've accomplished, it's because of the person I've become and I attribute this to the books and tapes I listen to.

DC: Retailing products. A recent Direct Sales Association survey said over 70% of people who join an MLM program do so because they love the products. Question, if you aren't selling products how can those people find you?

DN: Traditional business analysis: determine if you can create a positive cash flow before you begin and don't wait six to nine months until you discover the startling fact that you can't do what it takes in a specific program to make money on your part-time or full-time basis.

SO: Learning to improve communication skills. Actually be someone different than you were a year ago.

JS: Commitment! Dedication! Perseverance!

The most overrated activity in business is?
CB: The most overrated activity in business is talking.

RB: Retailing products. 95% of our population wants nothing to do with selling. If you lead with product, many people are not going to get the big picture of what this is about.

DC: Recruiting. Recruiting someone means nothing. It is activating them after you recruit them that matters.

DN: "Share the product with people, the product sells itself." I've never seen anything that sells itself. There's another one. It's the hype of, "We'll build it for you! We do all the work and you get all the money!" It's overrated because it just doesn't happen.

JS: Overemphasizing the income potential! Show "real" income projections that can be attained by the average person.

If you had to start your business all over again, what would you do differently?

CB: If I had to start my business all over again, I'd watch less TV and read fewer novels. I would also talk to more people and listen better.

RB: I would devote more time up front to getting to know the people running the network marketing companies. I'd find out what their vision is, where they are going and what they plan to accomplish and how. I'd make sure I understood their values

DN: I would have invested more time and energy in researching the real workings of the industry and business of network marketing. It would have made some difference, but perhaps not a great deal.
There have been major evolutionary changes in the industry in the last 11 years and particularly the last four or five. Some things take time.

JS: I would have started Network Marketing right out of college. I would also be more organized as far as keeping tax records, etc.

What was your worst business decision?
CB: Nothing comes to mind.

RB: My worst decision was when I first got started I tried to be something that I wasn't and I ended up making a lot of mistakes which cost a lot of money. Whatever you do, it's important to be yourself.

DC: The biggest mistake we all make in this industry is spending too much time with the wrong people and not enough time with the right people.

DN: My worst business decision was to get involved in a couple of partnerships that were really devastating.

SO: Taking the advice of a hired gun that Cell Tech had brought in during the summer of 1997. Whew!

JS: I loaned distributors money! In fact, I loaned out over $250,000 one month and never got it back! Finally one distributor paid me $6,000 of the $15,000 he owed me...after 8 years!
Never, never, never loan money to distributors unless you're prepared to lose it all! If they truly have a "burning" desire to succeed, they will find the money they need!

What was your best business decision?
CB: My best business decision was becoming a Nikken, Inc distributor.

RB: When I understood the concept of leverage and how by leveraging resources properly, you can get the exponential growth that's possible in this business.

DC: Joining New Image International.

DN: My best business decision was to get into network marketing as a career!

SO: Took a silly workshop, back in 1989, on public speaking. Shook me to the core, and was never the same after that.

JS: Meeting my wife and teaching her the business and then having two stepsons to teach them Network Marketing also.

What do you consider to be the main keys of your success?

CB: The main keys of my success are: Being led by God Almighty to do the things that have worked for me. Unconditional love for people.

RB: Understanding the people I'm working with and figuring out a way to bring value to them. I always try to figure out how I can be of service to people I may work with. When you focus on what you can bring them and their success, things seem to fall into place for you.

DC: (1)Determination to persist and not be denied, (2) My sincere love for people and belief in their untapped potential, (3) Systematic, step by step, unified training systems for ALL aspects of this business which can be duplicated throughout the organization.

I am not just talking about retailing and recruiting I am talking about each and every aspect of this business!

DN: My commitment to excellence backed by enthusiasm, hard work, and dogged persistence. As I have grown more experienced, I place a higher and higher value on character and integrity. I want to be fair with people and help others.

SO: Belief that we are the answer to health. Belief that I deserve to be the one. Belief that there is no other option.

JS: I have G.U.T.S. That's what I call a "Great Urge To Succeed!" I never give up! I have a "burning" desire to "go for it"!

What's your success philosophy?

CB: My success philosophy is built on the example of Jesus Christ who taught that we must serve others to be great.

RB: Treat other people as I would want to be treated. Understanding people and how to be of service to them is a great basis for any type of relationship.

DC: There are basically 7 aspects to our life: Spiritual, Family, Business, Social, Recreational, Financial, & Physical. The goal is to try to stay balanced in these 7 areas.

What good is money without family and friends to share it with, or good health?

I can be unbalanced spiritually. My pastor says some people are so heavenly minded that they are not earthly good!

The key as I see it is to do my best on a daily basis to stay in balance so I can be a source of courage and inspiration to other people. When all is said and done on this earth the only thing that really is going to matter is if you made a difference in the lives of others.

DN: Do unto others what you would have others do unto you. Your thoughts determine your actions. Create a strong vision, establish written goals, enthusiastically use a strong work ethic, and you can obtain whatever you truly want.

SO: Stop looking at your fears. Look where you are going, where you want to go. Objections are those scary bumps that appear when you take your eyes off your goal.

JS: The same as Henry Ford's, "To be successful in business, you must find a need and fill it!"

What about you has changed the most since finding success in business?
CB: What has changed, about me, the most since finding success in business is personal growth that enables me to help many people in various important ways including financially and spiritually.

RB: I am having more fun in my life. It's easier to appreciate life with money than without. And now I am able to make a difference with other people. I'm able to help them reach the lifestyle goals they have for themselves and I couldn't do this when I was chasing a paycheck myself.

Being able to help others live their dreams has been satisfying in ways I could not have imagined.

DC: Not a lot has changed, just no more financial stress. As I stated earlier money just makes you more of what you already are.

DN: I experience less stress and I enjoy each day more completely.

SO: My sense that I can do anything.

JS: I used to have my goals set on money. Now, I am focused on helping people live longer and healthier lives! After all, your health is your greatest wealth!

What is the legacy you hope to leave?
CB: The legacy I hope to leave is an example of one who was a channel of God's love to many needy people, starting with family, friends, and also to many I will never meet on this earth.

RB: That I treated everybody right and that I did the most with my opportunities.

DC: First I hope I will always be known as a loving father and husband. Next I would like to be known as someone who dreamed big and lived a life filled with passion.

Someone who always saw greatness in others and inspired them to reach deep inside and unleash their God given talents and abilities.

Lastly, I hope that one day it will be said that Dale Calvert and his leadership team at New Image International were instrumental in returning the network marketing industry to its roots of personal growth and leadership development.

DN: David Nelson was the "Champion of the Little Networker," he truly was the "Protector of the Part-Timer."

SO: That I played a role in clarifying, and simplifying, the principles of how health works. Sort of the Seven Habits of Highly Healthy People.

JS: I hope to be known for my devotion to helping develop "life-changing" products that help people live longer, pain-free healthy lives!

I also want to be able to provide an unending stream of residual income for my family including children, grandchildren, etc...so they can enjoy a good education and abundant wealth and happiness.

An Introduction to Network Marketing:
How It Works
by Gery Carson

Simply put, Network Marketing is just another business method of moving products and services from manufacturers to consumers - but with a twist. The twist is that it lets people like you and me in on the profits!

First, let's look at why more and more manufacturers, including Fortune 500 companies, are embracing Network Marketing.

Obviously, manufacturers want to get their products into the hands of as many people as possible, and as quickly as possible.

In conventional marketing, however, this may require millions of dollars of ongoing advertising expenses. It will also probably require going through layers of middlemen (jobbers, wholesalers, retailers, etc.) - each who want their cut of the profits (while adding ZERO value to the product or service). In addition, the competition can be fierce. And even after spending millions, there's no guarantee of success.

Now consider Network Marketing. In Network Marketing, the manufacturer introduces his product in the form of a business opportunity, much like a franchise, to a small nucleus of independent business people. The company will produce and supply the products at wholesale; provide the necessary promotional and sales materials; handle data processing and accounting; and even help in training.

This nucleus of people then introduce the products and business opportunity to others, who, in turn, introduce it to even more people. And so it continues - with the base of consumers and independent distributors growing larger and larger every year.

This partnership of the Network Marketing company and its independent distributors is of course mutually beneficial. The company slashes huge amounts of cash from its distribution and sales costs. The company doesn't have to advertise anymore either because its distributors do it for them - often just through "word of mouth."

And where do all the millions of dollars saved go? To the distributors, of course, in the form of commissions and overrides.But in contrast to conventional marketing, the company now only pays for results; i.e., commissions and overrides are paid out only when products are sold.

But since each individual can only personally move a small amount of product, Network Marketing companies also allow you to sponsor other people into the business and earn override commissions on their efforts, too.

This is one of the most powerful advantages that Network Marketing has over other traditional, direct-selling methods. You see, success in conventional direct selling usually means you have to be a super salesman and retail huge amounts of product. Network Marketing is just the opposite. Success in Network Marketing is about a lot of people each doing a little.

Also, unlike most traditional direct selling, Network Marketing isn't a job. On the contrary, it's your own business, to run as you like. And no matter when you join a Network Marketing organization, you start out as and will always be the head of your own company. You'll build your own network of independent distributors and earn a percentage of their sales. Yet each is a CEO in their own right, as you are, and each with the opportunity to build their own money-making networks under them.

Do you know what happens when you double a penny every day for a month? At the 15-day mark, it's grown to only $163.84. But by the 30th day, it's mushroomed to OVER 5 MILLION Dollars!

This duplication effect is the most powerful ingredient of Network Marketing. It's also the reason why Network Marketing is creating financial freedom for thousands of people worldwide today.

Imagine that you've shared your Network Marketing opportunity with John in Texas. John has an associate in Ohio by the name of Mark. Mark comes aboard and soon shares the opportunity with Jean from New York. Through Jean's efforts, a Californian, Rita, joins the network.

By just sponsoring one person, you've set into motion a chain of events that now has people working indirectly on your behalf across the United States! And every person (John, Mark, Jean, and Rita) is each adding to your commission check! This is just one very small example of duplication and networking in action.

Do you think you could find one person each month to join your business? Just one person a month who might be interested in financial freedom, more leisure time, more security, and more happiness?

Do you think you can teach that one person a month to do what you do? If you can, you can become wildly successful in Network Marketing!

But you know what? Even if you're only able to sponsor someone every 3-4 months, full-time incomes are still possible. And that's after just your first year. Consider what you can do in year two, year three, and beyond! ■

This article is an excerpt from the booklet
"The World's Greatest Home Based Business" by Gery Carson.

"The World's Greatest Home Based Business" is an engaging, easy-to-read layman's guide to understanding Network Marketing. WGHB will educate and excite your prospects about Network Marketing, shoot down misconceptions, and clearly show why Network Marketing is such an incredible business opportunity. Includes charts comparing network marketing to franchises, investments, etc. Also includes common questions and answers.

16 glossy full-color pages. WGHB booklets are inexpensive (as little as 27¢ apiece), lightweight, and fit perfectly in a #10 envelope. WGHB also includes an order form that allows readers, if desired, to order the excellent Network Marketing "why-to" book, Future Choice and/or a leading Network Marketing introductory video. For those who wish to engage in further "due diligence," this gives them an easy, no-hassle way to do just that (at no hassle or additional cost to you!).

For a sample copy, send $1.00 to Carson Services, Inc., PO Box 4785, Lincoln, NE 68504. Request item no. L150. WGHB can also be found on the Web at:

www.networkmarketing.com/intro.html

RESOURCES
Recommended by Gery Carson

General Printing...
PRESS AMERICA, INC.
661 Fargo Avenue
Elk Grove Village, IL 60007 USA
Ph: (847) 228-0333   Fax: (847) 228-7333
Website: www.pressamerica.com

BUDGET SIGNS & PRINTING
2765 W. Jefferson   Suite H
Springfield, IL 62702 USA
Ph: (217) 546-2737

Envelopes...
BUSINESS ENVELOPES
Mid-Atlantic Industrial Park
PO Box 517
Thorofare, NJ 08086-0517 USA
Ph: (800) 275-4400   Fax: (800) 605-5162

HEINRICH ENVELOPE
2905 Heinrich Drive
Boone, IA 50036 USA
Ph: (800) 383-1262   Fax: (515) 432-2454
Contact Person: Steve Fridholm

Full-Color Printing...
U.S. PRESS
1628A James P. Rodgers Drive
Valdosta, GA 31601 USA
Ph: (800) 631-8507   Fax: (912) 247-4405

CUTTING EDGE PRINTING
29 South Market St.
Elizabethtown, PA 17022 USA
Ph: (800) 561-9297   Fax: (717) 361-0860
Website: www.mlmprinting.com

Audio Cassette Duplication...
CASSETTE DUPLICATORS, INC.
2211 West Printers Row, 2300 So.
Salt Lake City, UT 84119 USA
Contact Person: Doug Wilson
Ph: (800) 829-0077   Fax: (801) 977-0120

Mailing Lists...
CUTTING EDGE MEDIA
29 South Market St.
Elizabethtown, PA 17022 USA
Ph: (717) 361-9007   Fax: (717) 361-0860
Website: www.cuttingedgemedia.com

Website Promotion...
http://selfpromotion.com/?CF=Gery%20Carson

(be sure to type the URL exactly as shown, the "Gery Carson" part tells 'em I sent you)

This site will provide you with some great education about search engines and it's also one of the places we endorse for inexpensive site registration.

Voice Mail...
CARSON SERVICES, INC.
PO Box 4785
Lincoln, NE 68504 USA
Ph: (402) 434-8480   Fax: (402)-467-4292
EMail: Mail@carsonsi.com
Website: www.carsonsi.com

Graphics/Clip Art...
DYNAMIC GRAPHICS, INC.
6000 N. Forest Park Dr
Peoria, IL 61614 USA
Ph: (309) 688-8800   Fax: (309) 688-3075

Advertising (business opportunities)...
CUTTING EDGE MEDIA
29 South Market St.
Elizabethtown, PA 17022 USA
Ph: (717) 361-9007   Fax: (717) 361-0860
Website: www.cuttingedgemedia.com

MONEY 'N PROFITS Magazine
28 Veset St. #242
New York, NY 10007 USA
Ph: (212) 785-9080   Fax: (212) 785-8007

WOLF ENTERPRISES (Advertising Agency)
104 Cassidy Ct.
Cary, NC 27511 USA
Ph: (919) 481-2126   Fax: (919) 380-8013

Websites...
www.sixfigureincome.com
www.profitsonline.com
www.networkmarketing.com
www.fortunenow.com
www.mlmu.com

Office Supplies...
QUILL CORPORATION
PO Box 94080
Palantine, IL 60094 USA
Ph: (800) 789-8965   Fax: (800) 789-8955
Website: www.quillcorp.com

Fax-on-Demand Service...
CARSON SERVICES, INC.
PO Box 4785
Lincoln, NE 68504 USA
Ph: (402) 434-8480   Fax: (402)-467-4292
EMail: Mail@carsonsi.com
Website: www.carsonsi.com

Computers...
APPLE MACINTOSH
Ph: 800-538-9696
Website: www.apple.com
Despite Microsoft's attempts to copy the look and feel of the Mac with Windows, Mac is still far and away the easiest and most fun computer to use. The Mac has been instrumental in my success, and I strongly recommend it as a business computer! And with Apple's cool new iMacs and G3's, there isn't a better value available in desktop computing.

Computer Software...
There are thousands of software programs available for Macintosh. Here are some I LOVE and use daily:

- AppleWorks (word processing, database, & spreadsheets)
- FileMaker Pro (database)
- Netscape Navigator (Web browsing)
- Quark Express (Page design/layout)
- Adobe PhotoShop
- Adobe CyberStudio (Website design)
- Adobe ImageReady
- Quicken or QuickBooks (accounting)
- BBEdit

These and thousands of other Mac programs can be ordered at the following Mac Websites:
www.macconnection.com
www.macmall.com
www.warehouse.com
www.zones.com

Network Marketing Training...
UPLINE
400 E. Jefferson St.
Charlottesville, VA 22902 USA
Ph: (804) 979-4427   Fax: (804) 979-1602
Website: www.upline.com

KAAS PUBLISHING
1199 E. Nasa Rd. One #104
Houston, TX 77058
Ph: (281) 280-9800   Fax: (281) 486-0549
Website: www.fortunenow.com & www.fortunenow.com

KIM KLAVER
4741 Central #300
Kansas City, MO 64112 USA
Ph: (816) 333-6619 Fax: (816) 333-6615

Ad Copywriting...
TREVOR LEVINE
3284 Adeline St., Suite B
Berkeley, CA 94703 USA
Ph: (510) 547-7810
Email: Levine@marketingexperts.com
Website: marketingexperts.com

Network Marketing Consultation...
KEVIN JANNAIN
615 Main St. #135
Stroudsburg, PA 18360 USA
Ph: (717) 629-7889 Fax: (717) 629-0658

DEBBI BALLARD
2815 S Alma School RD Ste 119A
Mesa, AZ 85210
Ph: (602) 831-3024 Fax: (602) 839-5706

Network Marketing Legal Counsel...
JEFFREY A. BABENER
121 SW Morrison, Suite 1020
Portland, OR 97204 USA
Ph: (503) 226-6600 Fax: (503) 226-4290

GERALD P. NEHRA
1710 Beach Street
Muskegon, MI 49441 USA
Ph: (616) 755-3800 and 616-755-8200 Fax (616) 755-4700
Website: www.mlmatty.com

D. JACK SMITH
5100 Poplar Ave. #2700
Memphis, TN 38137 USA
Ph: (901) 685-7299 Fax: (901) 763-2976
Website: www.vrfirst.com/jack

To **Contact** Our Interviewees...

Brian Biro
204 Weston Way
Asheville, NC 28803
Ph: 828-654-8852
Fax: 828-654-8853
bbiro@worldnet.att.net

Robert Blackman
PO Box 1390
Norman, OK 73070
Ph: 405-360-9487
Fax: 405-360-9489
Robert1MLM@aol.com

Chuck Branham
PO Box 535
Graham, WA 98338
Ph: 360-893-3580
Fax: 360-893-3680
cncbranham@unidial.com

Robert Butwin
1051 Slate Drive
Santa Rosa, CA 95405
Ph: 707-537-1042
Fax: 707-537-1083
butwin@mindspring.com

Dale Calvert
Calvert Marketing
119 Merganser Ct.
Georgetown, KY 40324
Fax: 502-867-0629
DTCalvert@aol.com

Marty Challenger
201 Kenwood Court
Novato, CA 94945
Ph: 800-818-3688
Fax: 415-892-4947
cstclubvac@aol.com

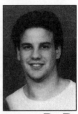

Thomas DeRosa
61 Thorson Rd.
Oxford, CT 06478
Ph: 203-881-1037
Fax: 203-881-1091
Tom@bostononline.net

Tracy Dieterich
Coppell, Texas
Ph: 800-938-0607
tracyd@ausa.net

Rick Eriksen
21712 Wesley Dr #2
Laguna Beach, CA 92651
Ph: 949-499-3707
Fax: 949-499-5031
eriksen2@home.com

Tony Kent
Arroyo Hondo
Santa Fe, NM 87505
Ph: 505-982-2022
Fax: 505-983-2232
tkent@trail.com

Charles Leslie
3420 Sandy Cir Dr
Bellingham, WA 98225
Ph: 360-671-9511
Fax: 360-738-7206
eagle@pacificrim.net

Trevor Levine
3284 Adeline St, Suite B
Berkeley, CA 94703-2439
Ph: 510-547-7810
levine@marketingexperts.com

Jim McAfee
1271 High St
Auburn, CA 95603
Ph: 530-823-7092
Fax: 530-823-7086
jmcafee@jps.net

David A. Nelson
7270 S Hudson Way
Littleton, CO 80122
Ph: 303-694-4151

Scott Ohlgren
2556 County Road 204
Durango, CO 81301-7712
Ph: 800-797-3912

Joe Rubino
68 Park Street
Andover, MA 01810
Ph: 978-470-0050 or 800-999-9551 X870
Fax: 978-887-3126
jrubino@bigfoot.com

Jim Strickland
PO Box 5647
Destin, FL 32540
Ph: 850-654-7260
Fax: 850-654-7250
admin@naturesgold.com

SECRETS
for building the
$100,000
home-based business

Want giant, bank account-bursting income? Then you better be emulating giant, bank account-bursting income earners! And NOBODY gives you the scoop on more six-figure-earning home business entrepreneurs than Six-Figure Income Magazine.

● We show you who's making the big bucks in home business. More importantly, SFI shows you <u>HOW</u> they're making it – the attitude, the philosophies, the actual techniques used by some of the most savvy, intelligent, and dynamic entrepreneurs on the planet. You get exact strategies, secrets, tips, and worldly-wise advice you can start using <u>right</u> <u>now</u> to build your own personal fortune at home.

● You'll learn from the masters what real freedom is all about - the money to live your dreams...and the time to actually live them!

● <u>For</u> <u>less</u> <u>than</u> <u>$5</u> <u>a</u> <u>month</u>, you'll enjoy full, <u>insider</u> <u>access</u> to the kind of information that these movers and shakers normally charge <u>thousands</u> <u>of</u> <u>dollars</u> for.

● SFI gives you a direct pipeline to the minds of the home business super-rich and <u>it's</u> <u>available</u> <u>NOWHERE</u> <u>ELSE!</u> Every article in SFI is an <u>exclusive</u> –every issue a recipe for turning your small business into a BIG paycheck.

Missing a single issue could be hazardous to your wealth!

Call *402-434-8480* to order your subscription today
or order on the Web at: *www.sixfigureincome.com*

The Home Business Revolution's Greatest Entrepreneurs *makes a great gift for friends who work at home or are thinking about starting a home-based business.*

Are you a network marketer? Get a copy for all your downline associates.

Brian Biro
Robert Blackman
Chuck Branham
Robert Butwin
Dale Calvert
Marty Challenger
Thomas DeRosa
Tracy Dieterich
Rick Eriksen
Tony Kent
Charles Leslie
Trevor Levine
Jim McAfee
David Nelson
Scott Ohlgren
Joe Rubino
Jim Strickland

The exclusive interviews from Six-Figure Income Magazine
GERY CARSON with Jan Wallen

Quantity:	Price:
1 copy	$17.95 each
2-5 copies.........................	$15.95 each
6-24 copies........................	$12.95 each
25 - 49 copies.....................	$9.95 each

Call for larger quantities

Add Shipping & Handling to above prices:
– US and Canada residents add $2 for first book; $.50 for each additional book.
– Residents of other countries add 30% of total book cost.

Order by calling **402-434-8480**
or order on the Web at: **www.sixfigureincome.com**

Mail orders can be sent to:

Carson Services, Inc., PO Box 4785, Lincoln, NE 68504 USA.

Cash, check, money order, or charge accepted. Make checks to: Carson Services, Inc.

ALL PRICES SUBJECT TO CHANGE WITHOUT NOTICE